Misery

by Stephen King

Adapted for the stage by
Simon Moore

Samuel French — London
New York - Toronto - Hollywood

© 1999 BY STEPHEN KING AND SIMON MOORE

Rights of Performance by Amateurs are controlled by Samuel French Ltd, 52 Fitzroy Street, London W1P 6JR, and they, or their authorized agents, issue licences to amateurs on payment of a fee. **It is an infringement of the Copyright to give any performance or public reading of the play before the fee has been paid and the licence issued.**

The Royalty Fee indicated below is subject to contract and subject to variation at the sole discretion of Samuel French Ltd.

Basic fee for each and every
performance by amateurs   Code M
in the British Isles

The Professional Repertory Rights in this play are controlled by Samuel French Ltd

---

The publication of this play does not imply that it is necessarily available for performance by amateurs or professionals, either in the British Isles or Overseas. Amateurs and professionals considering a production are strongly advised in their own interests to apply to the appropriate agents for written consent before starting rehearsals or booking a theatre or hall.

ISBN 0 573 01850 2

Please see page iv for further copyright information

MISERY

Presented by Brian Eastman and Andrew Welch for Carnival Theatre at the Criterion Theatre, London, on 17th December 1992, with the following cast:

Paul Sheldon	Bill Paterson
Annie Wilkes	Sharon Gless

Directed by **Simon Moore**
Designed by **Patrick Connellan**
Lighting by **Tim Mitchell**
Music by **Gavin Greenaway**

COPYRIGHT INFORMATION

(See also page ii)

This play is fully protected under the Copyright Laws of the British Commonwealth of Nations, the United States of America and all countries of the Berne and Universal Copyright Conventions.

All rights including Stage, Motion Picture, Radio, Television, Public Reading, and Translation into Foreign Languages, are strictly reserved.

No part of this publication may lawfully be reproduced in ANY form or by any means — photocopying, typescript, recording (including video-recording), manuscript, electronic, mechanical, or otherwise—or be transmitted or stored in a retrieval system, without prior permission.

Licences for amateur performances are issued subject to the understanding that it shall be made clear in all advertising matter that the audience will witness an amateur performance; that the names of the authors of the plays shall be included on all programmes; and that the integrity of the authors' work will be preserved.

The Royalty Fee is subject to contract and subject to variation at the sole discretion of Samuel French Ltd.

In Theatres or Halls seating Four Hundred or more the fee will be subject to negotiation.

In Territories Overseas the fee quoted above may not apply. A fee will be quoted on application to our local authorized agent, or if there is no such agent, on application to Samuel French Ltd, London.

VIDEO-RECORDING OF AMATEUR PRODUCTIONS

Please note that the copyright laws governing video-recording are extremely complex and that it should not be assumed that any play may be video-recorded for whatever purpose without first obtaining the permission of the appropriate agents. The fact that a play is published by Samuel French Ltd does not indicate that video rights are available or that Samuel French Ltd controls such rights.

CHARACTERS

Paul, middle-aged
Annie, middle-aged

ACT I
SCENE 1	The Twenty-sixth Annual Romantic Fiction Awards. Winter
SCENE 2	A Colorado farmhouse. Morning. Winter
SCENE 3	The same. Night
SCENE 4	The same. Night
SCENE 5	The same. Day
SCENE 6	The same. Night
SCENE 7	The same
SCENE 8	The same. Two days later
SCENE 9	The same. Christmas morning
SCENE 10	The same. Morning

ACT II
SCENE 1	The farmhouse. Day. Spring
SCENE 2	The same. Day
SCENE 3	The same. Night
SCENE 4	The same. Day
SCENE 5	The same. Night
SCENE 6	The same. Night
SCENE 7	The same. Late Spring
SCENE 8	The same. Night
SCENE 9	The same. Morning
SCENE 10	The Twenty-eighth Annual Romantic Fiction Awards

Time: the present

Billing requirement

Presenting companies, either professional repertory or amateur, must adhere to the following billing requirement:

The name of Simon Moore shall be prominently and legibly announced as the Adapter of the said play following immediately after the title and the Author Stephen King on all programmes, posters, printing and other advertising matter in connection with the said play and where it is practicable to do so having regard to space available on all theatre signs and marquees in a size and boldness of type not less than that accorded to the Director of the said play. There shall be no use of the style "Stephen King's *Misery*" or any similar possessory credit save that a reference to the said play being based on Stephen King's *Misery* will be permissible. The Author's credit shall be no more prominent and no larger than the credit for any other member of the creative team.

ACT I

Winter

SCENE 1

Twenty-sixth Annual Romantic Fiction Awards

A microphone stands down stage; a giant cut-out of a romantic novel "Misery's Child, by Paul Sheldon" behind it. The cover shows a nineteenth century heroine with windswept hair, voluptuous but vulnerable, in the arms of a dashing young hero. Behind them is another, older man, grey haired but vigorous and attractive

There is huge applause as Paul, an attractive middle-aged man, stands in front of the microphone, hugging a large bronze award in the shape of a rose. He is wearing an expensive suit, and has a relaxed, confident manner: this is not the first time he's won an award. He has a little index card with notes on, which he sneaks a look at from time to time

Flashbulbs are going off all the time

Paul Thank you, thank you for this... Thank you.

He waits for the applause to subside

I want to dedicate this, this wonderful award, to you ladies. And maybe a few of your husbands, if they're honest enough to admit they read me too. When I sit down to write a book, you're the people I do it for. It's as simple as that. You know, it's become very fashionable to ridicule romantic fiction. But in this world of ... of chaos, and violence, I don't think we can have too much romance, do you?

Applause. He lifts the statuette, kisses it

The question that everyone always asks writers is "Where do you get all your ideas from?" Everywhere I go, I get the same question. If I ever get to heaven, St Peter's going to stop me at the gates and say "Hey Paul, where do you get all the ideas from?" Well, ten years ago, when I got the biggest idea of my life, I ran away to a little hotel in Colorado, and wrote all winter,

2   Misery

and the result was the first of the Misery novels. When I leave here today, I'm going to go to that same hotel, and no, ladies, (*he smiles*) I'm not telling you where it is, and I'm going to sit in the same room, and write on the same hotel typewriter. And the day I finish I'll smoke a single cigarette and drink a bottle of Dom Perignon, just as I've done every year, and you'll have the new Paul Sheldon. I just hope you like it as much as the others. Thank you truly, and I'll see you when the snow melts!

Applause. He starts to go and then stops

I forgot the whole point of what I was going to say! Ideas! I was going to tell you where ideas come from. Ten years ago, halfway between my first divorce and my second divorce...

Laughter

...I was on a plane from Munich to Denver for a sales conference, and I was very depressed. There was a woman next to me reading a newspaper, and I was reading over her shoulder, like you do. There was a small piece about tourists stranded in the Bahamas because of some airport strike, and the headline was "Misery in Paradise". And I became fixated by that headline. I was not a writer until that exact moment. I never went to the sales conference, I resigned from my job. Because I'd had an idea that wouldn't go away. And the idea was: what if Misery was a *person*?

The audience applauds wildly. Paul soaks it up. In the background we can hear a low, ugly noise, a whine. It starts to get louder and louder until it drowns the applause

SCENE 2

A Colorado farmhouse. Morning

Lights like car headlamps blind us as the almost deafening noise continues. It sounds like a car horn being pressed continuously. As the sound and light slowly die away, they are replaced by gentle birdsong and soft dawn light beginning to illuminate a small bedroom in a wooden farmhouse

We see the cut-away front of the house showing a hall, downstairs bedroom, bathroom, front door with several large locks, kitchen and front garden. All of them share a claustrophobic, neglected feel. Rickety stairs in the hallway lead up to an attic bedroom (the interior of which is not seen) and down to a cellar (again unseen)

Act I, Scene 2

3

There is an ugly tree outside, which has grown much too near the house, and now seems to be part of it, winding itself round the side of the building, spreading and growing into the roof itself like some alien parasite. Thick snow has covered the farmhouse—a path has been cut away to allow access to the front door. It's still snowing heavily, and the overall effect is like a gingerbread cottage in a fairy story

The furnishings are contradictory: flowered covers and lamp shades compete with bare, rusting pipes and naked light bulbs. It's like the home of someone who can be very neat one moment, and a shameless slob the next

Part of the bedroom has been turned over to a working area, with a small wooden bench. There are glass jars with combs of honey stacked against the wall

As the morning light slowly fills the room, we become aware that there is a man, Paul, asleep in the bed. To the side of the bed is an intravenous drip, not connected up

Sitting absolutely still on the other side of the room is a middle-aged woman, Annie, stockily built. She is expressionless, watching him

Somewhere out of sight a TV is on, tuned to a home shopping channel, too low to really hear properly

Paul starts to stir in the bed. He is mumbling. He wakes up and tries unsuccessfully to sit up

Annie (*gently*) Don't do that, Paul. If you get those legs of yours talking again, they won't shut up. And I can't give you any more pills yet. I'm giving you too much as it is.
Paul (*half-asleep, confused*) I can't do anything. (*He looks at her blankly for a moment*)
Annie You remember who I am? Yes you do. I'm Annie Wilkes. I've told you enough times.
Paul How did I get here?
Annie By a miracle. There's no other word to describe it.
Paul (*shaking his head*) I can't remember.
Annie There was a storm, but all the weathermen were saying it was going to go south towards New Mexico. I was in Sidewinder, getting feed for the livestock. Andy Roberts said I'd better step on it if I was going to get back here before the storm hit, and I said to Andy, "That storm is going south". But he said, "No, it's changed its mind". I had to get back, there's no-one to feed the animals but me. The nearest people are the Roydmans, and

4 Misery

they're miles away, and boy, they don't like me. (*She suddenly switches off for a second, like a robot that's suffered a total power cut. She just stares vacantly into space*)

Paul looks at her—what should he do?

Then Annie comes back and carries on as if nothing at all has happened

I got about five miles out and the snow started. It came fast—up here it always does. I was just creeping along with my lights on, and then I saw the skid marks! An hour later and the snow would have covered them up completely. If I'd been on an upgrade, I might not have stopped. Not very Christian, I know, but there were three inches on the road already and even with a four wheel drive you can't be sure of getting going again. I stopped and looked over the edge and then I saw your car all topsy-turvy, half-buried in the snow down by the river. I hoofed it down through the trees and then I heard groaning. That was you, Paul.

Paul I don't remember any of this.

Annie When I pulled you out you had that little bruise on your head but that didn't look like anything. It was your legs! (*She winces*) I could see straight away that your legs just weren't—right.

Paul looks down nervously to where his legs are covered by the blankets, but doesn't dare move the sheets to look yet

I knew I had to get you in the warm or you'd die. So I dragged you up into the truck—you weighed a ton! You're lucky I don't give up easy—and drove home as fast as I dared. (*She shakes her head*) I could smell the booze on your breath, Paul.

That triggers more memories

Paul I'd been drinking champagne—because I'd finished the book. I was so stupid...

Annie Stupid is the word, Paul. I was sure you were going to die... I mean, I was so sure! And then you screamed, and I felt better because I knew you'd live. So I gave you some strong pain medication and then you went to sleep. Then you woke up and started to scream again, and I gave you some more. (*She moves over to the bed and sits on the edge, gives him a sip of water from a glass by the bed*) While you were out I got your driver's licence, and I saw the name Paul Sheldon, and I thought, "Oh, that must be a coincidence"... But then I went into the hall, and checked the picture on the back of *Misery in France*, and then I got scared, I got real scared and

Act I, Scene 2 5

I had to sit down, I thought I was going to faint. Then I found your Writer's Guild card, and I knew you were Paul Sheldon. Oh boy, oh boy! *The* Paul Sheldon!

Paul (*smiling*) I'm amazed you know who I am.

Annie That's a laugh! I'm your number one fan! *Your number one fan!* That's what's so ... miraculous. Before I got the feed I went to check out the paperbacks at Wilson's. I was hoping *Misery's Child* would be out finally, but no such luck. Paul, I was actually *thinking* about you.

Paul tries to move and winces. She gives him another sip of water

You ran a fever for a while, but I knocked that out with some Keflex. You had one or two close calls. You've been unconscious most of the last two weeks. You owe me your life.

Paul is starting to really understand what's happened

Paul Two weeks? I've been out two weeks?

Annie I fed you intravenously to start with—that's what the marks on your arms are.

Paul Shouldn't I uh ... be in a hospital?

Annie You're better than in hospital! Because I'm a trained nurse! You won't get finer care anywhere. Now it's time you rested. (*She stands up*)

Paul My legs really hurt.

Annie Of course they do. In a minute you can have some more medication.

Paul (*eagerly*) Yes, I think I need some now.

Annie Any minute. Don't tire yourself by talking too much. (*She makes to leave the room*)

Paul suddenly remembers something terribly important

Paul Did you find a bag? In the car——

Annie (*shaking her head*) What kind of bag?

Paul's face drops. Then Annie grins, opens the bedside dresser and pulls out an old soft leather briefcase

You mean this? I was just fooling with you, you old silly.

Paul is very relieved. She playfully holds it from his reach

I took the liberty of looking inside it. You don't mind, do you?

Paul No, no, of course not. I'm just relieved you've got it.

6   Misery

She pulls out a typed manuscript and holds it to her breast like a lover. Then she looks at him slyly, like a coy child trying to guess her birthday present before she opens it

Annie It's called *Fast Cars* … so it can't be a Misery novel. No cars in the nineteenth century, fast or otherwise! I took the liberty of glancing through it—you don't mind, do you?

Paul Of course not.

Annie And if I read it? You wouldn't mind?

Paul (*smiling*) You're privileged—you'll be the first person in the world to read it apart from me.

Annie Because I would never presume to do such a thing without your permission. I respect you too much. In fact, Paul, I love you. (*She suddenly becomes very embarrassed*) Your creativity—that's all I meant.

Paul I know. You're my number one fan.

She lights up

Annie That's it! That's it exactly! You wouldn't mind if I read it in the spirit of fan-love?

Paul No.

Annie I'm sorry it's not a Misery book—I hope you don't mind me saying that.

Paul laughs, and even that small movement makes him feel the pain again

Paul It's better than the Misery books. Much better, actually. I've been planning this for the last five years. I happen to think it's the best work I've ever done.

Annie (*sincerely*) Then it must be truly great, Paul.

Paul Well, I don't know about that. But let's just say you may be looking at the winner of next year's American Book Award.

Annie sighs with deep pleasure

Annie You're good. I knew you would be. Just reading your books I knew you would be. A man who could think of Misery Chastain, who could breathe life into someone like her, just had to be good.

Paul I wonder if you could make a telephone call for me? My agent is going to be very worried about me.

Annie Of course. But the phone lines are down at the moment because of the snow. (*She checks her watch*) Time for your pills! Two every six hours. On the hour. (*She grins*) On the hour—not before, not five minutes to the hour, but on the hour.

Act I, Scene 3

She puts the capsules in his mouth and makes him suck them off her fingers. She holds the glass of water to his lips

Paul Is this a farm? I've heard animals.

Annie Not really. Half a dozen laying hens, two cows ... oh, and Misery. (*She laughs*) You won't think I'm very nice, calling a sow after the brave, beautiful woman you created. But I meant no disrespect. She's very friendly. (*She wrinkles her nose up and suddenly becomes a sow, and makes pig like sounds*) Whoink! Whoink! Whoink!

He watches her grunting. Annie walks out of the room, still grunting

Whoink! Whoink! Whoink! Whoink!

Fade to darkness

SCENE 3

The same. Night

The house is dark apart from a few small, shaded lights

Annie is sitting on the edge of the bed, feeding Paul soup. Nothing but the sound of him slurping. She gives him a spoonful, then waits a few moments just like a nurse. The silence becomes oppressive and he tries to make conversation

Paul You haven't mentioned the book. Have you read any of it?

She smiles in a half-hearted way, looks confused

Annie About forty pages. (*She pauses*) I don't think it's as good as the others. It's hard to follow. It keeps jumping about in time.

Paul It's just a technique—it shows Tony's confused state of mind——

Annie Yes, he's very confused, and that makes it less interesting. Not boring—I'm sure you couldn't create a boring character. But ... less interesting.

Paul Well, it's a style a lot of contemporary novels use, it's called stream-of-consciousness.

Annie (*unimpressed*) Is it?

He swallows another mouthful. She's still holding back

8   Misery

Paul What else?

Annie Well, Paul ... it's the profanity! Every other word is that—effword!
(*She searches for the right phrase*) It has... It has no nobility!

Paul Tony's a ghetto kid from Spanish Harlem, and everyone uses those
words——

Annie They do *not*! What do you think I say when I go to the feed store in
town? What do you think I say? "Now Andy, give me a bag of that effing
pigfeed and a bag of that bitchly cow-corn and some of that Christing ear-
mite medicine"? And what do you think he says to me? "You're effing
right, Annie, coming right the eff up"? (*She's angry, shaking the soup bowl
she's holding*) And then I suppose I go down the street to the bank and say
to Mrs Bollinger "Here's one big bastard of a cheque and you better give
me fifty effing dollars just as effing quick as you can"? Do you think that
when they put me on the stand in Denver and accused— (*She spills some
soup on the coverlet*) There! Look what you've made me do!

Paul Look, Annie, I'm sorry you don't like the book.

Annie It wasn't what I wanted!

Paul Well, I'm sorry about that.

Annie Misery's what I like! Misery! Not some foul little spic car-thief! (*She
suddenly throws the bowl on the floor and turns off completely. Just sits
there for twenty seconds completely unaware of the outside world*)

*Paul watches her, terrified of moving. Then Annie gives a small laugh and
suddenly she's back again*

I have such a temper.

Paul I'm sorry.

Annie You should be. (*She stands up*) You don't use those words in the
Misery books because ... they weren't even invented then! Animal times
breed animal words, I suppose. But you ought to stick to your Misery
stories, Paul. I say that sincerely. As your Number One Fan. (*She calms
down*) I blacked out all the swear words with a pen for you.

Paul (*after a pause*) Thanks.

Annie I may go back to it later.

Paul Don't do that if it makes you angry. I sort of depend on you, you know.

Annie You sure do.

Paul Is the, uh, telephone working yet?

Annie It's not, Paul, no.

Paul Only it's been quite——

Annie I am aware of how long the telephone has been out, and I'd rather you
didn't keep quizzing me about it. I'm not the phone company, Paul. (*She
shakes her head and starts to leave the room*)

Paul Annie——

Act I, Scene 4   9

Annie What?!
Paul Uh, I have a pack of cigarettes in my bag——
Annie I know you do, Paul. They're cancer sticks.
Paul (*lightly*) So they say. I wonder if I could have them?
Annie No. I don't want your death on my conscience. (*She shakes her head*)
And you, still so ill! Smokers! (*She shakes her head again, as if she just
can't believe his stupidity*)

Annie leaves the room, leaving soup all over the floor

Paul You're not mad at me, are you, Annie? (*He waits, wondering what to
do, getting more and more anxious*)

The Lights slowly fade to darkness

SCENE 4

The same. Night

A naked light bulb in the hall comes on

*Annie is standing in the hallway, turning the light on and off five times, every
five seconds. She has a bucket and a soapy rag*

*When it comes on, the light half-illuminates Paul, wide awake in bed in his
room. He's beginning to wonder what kind of place he's staying in*

*Annie is lit from above only, and she looks very, very weird. She is staring into
space, unaware of what she's doing. Suddenly, she turns the hall light off and
the main light comes on in Paul's room, momentarily blinding him. She's
back*

Annie I suppose you want your cockadoodie medication now.
Paul Oh, yes, please, I feel awful—I haven't slept at all. I never realized how
much they were dulling the pain.
Annie I have them. But first I have to clean up the mess on the floor. The mess
you made. (*She kneels on the floor and mops up the soup. For a while, she
cleans without talking to him or looking at him*)

He gets a bit angry with this game

Paul I wonder if I could have my tablets now?

10   Misery

Annie (*ignoring him*) I must rinse. Or else the soap will leave a dull spot. (*She obsessively cleans the floor*)

Paul Please Annie, the pain, I'm dying.

Annie You're not *dying*. (*She looks at him like a mother might look at a demanding kid in a supermarket*)

Paul You've made me wait nearly eight hours. I'm going to scream in a minute.

Annie Then scream. But remember, it's nobody's fault but your own. (*She finishes cleaning and stands up, produces some pills from her pocket*) Three Novril. Here. Three instead of your usual two.

He takes them gratefully

Wait. (*She reaches down and fills his glass half-full with the soupy, soapy, dirty water from the bucket*) Wash them down with this.

Paul can't believe what she's just said

I know you can dry swallow them, but please believe me when I say I can make them come right back up again.

He looks at her incredulously. This is unreal

Come on. It's only rinse water. It won't hurt you.

Paul There's no way I'm going to drink that! What do you think I am, some kind of naughty child? You must be joking.

Annie I assure you I am not joking, Paul. I will bring them back up again, just as——

His hand goes to his mouth

Paul!

Her voice stops him. His hand hovers, and then moves away from his mouth. He looks at the glass—there are bits of sediment floating in it. He really wants the pills. And he's frightened of her. She's serious. He takes the glass from her. He swallows the pills and takes a nominal sip

All of it.

He stares at her. She is tensing up—if he doesn't do what she says then something much worse will happen. Paul drinks from the glass and starts to gag

Act I, Scene 5   11

I wouldn't throw them up, Paul. No more until tomorrow.

She waits until he finishes the whole glass, then she slams it on the dresser beside the bed

(*Smiling*) You won't make me mad again, will you?
Paul No.

She kisses him on the cheek

Annie I love you.

Annie leaves the room with the bucket and turns out the light. She puts the bucket in the kitchen before going upstairs

Paul lies in bed, illuminated only by moonlight, the criss-cross pattern of the trees outside all over the walls of his room. He looks furious

He hears Annie's clumping footfalls as she goes to bed upstairs. Then the sound of her urinating. The flush. In the attic, two tiny windows light up like eyes

Paul finally plucks up courage and pulls the blanket back so that he can look at his legs. And then he moans aloud in horror: the lower parts of both legs are bound with slim steel rods, wrapped up with tape and bandages and wire. His thighs are covered in ugly, dark bruises

Paul Oh, Jesus Christ.

Black-out

SCENE 5

The same. A bright winter day

The Lights come up on Paul's room

Annie comes into the room in her huge old parka, shaking off snow and producing a paperback from her shopping bag. She is so excited

Annie They had it! In the store! That's why I've been so long! I opened it just to read the first page and before I knew what had happened I'd lost

12   Misery

myself and I was on page fifty and I realized you'd probably be screaming
out for your pills!

Paul I could do with them, sure. What have you been reading?

Annie *Misery's Child* of course, stupid! They got the paperback today!

Paul Right. (*He smiles*) It seems so long since I wrote it—I always think of
the hardback release as the time when——

Annie Yes, well, not everybody can afford fancy hardbacks, Mister Man!

Paul Well? Do you like it?

Whatever else, Paul hasn't lost his vanity

Annie Oh Paul, I *love* it. It's as good as all the rest. Better! The best! It more
than makes up for that other book.

Paul (*annoyed*) Thanks.

Annie I *knew* Misery would marry Rory, and I'm sure Baron Heidzig will
forgive Misery for marrying Rory, even though they were engaged. Does
he forgive her? No, don't tell! I want to find out for myself. I'm making it
last. It always seems so long before there's another one. I shan't sleep until
I finish it! (*She gives him his tablets*)

He eagerly swallows them and his relief is immediate

I've brought you chips and candy and extra pills because I'm not going to
do anything else until I've read to the end!

Paul That's great. Did you make that call for me, in town?

Annie I didn't get a chance. I'm sorry, but it's not every day you get the new
Paul Sheldon! Oh, which is your favourite? Out of all the ones you've
written?

Paul's heart sinks. She's never going to ring

Paul (*flatly*) I don't really have favourites. To be perfectly honest——

Annie I love them all, of course, but if I had to pick one … oh, it's so hard!
The one I've read the most, it's got to be *Misery Wronged*, where she's
kidnapped by the awful Black John Weston… And the most exciting is
probably *Misery in France*, where Rory rescued her at the very last minute
from the guillotine of the mad Count Leroux, and they escaped in that great
big balloon! But the most romantic one—no, the scariest one is definitely
Misery in Love, when she gets stripped of her title and thrown in the
horrible Bedlam hospital by her mad sister Gwendolyne Chastain… Ugh!

Paul can't help laughing—she's clearly such a fan

You see I was a nurse, so I know how terrible those places can be! You're

Act I, Scene 5

13

wonderful, Paul. You're just wonderful. (*She looks at the book again and again, like she can't believe it's hers*)

Paul What kind of nurse were you?

Annie Oh, all kinds. I worked in an old people's home for a few years, but that … that was very annoying… And then there was all that Denver business.

Paul (*nervously*) What was that, Annie?

Annie Oh, tell me what happens, Paul! (*She clutches the book tightly*) I've just got to the bit where Misery gets trapped by the gypsy fortune teller who's not really a gypsy fortune teller! Is it Gwendolyne? I'm sure it's that oogy woman! Is it? Is it?

Paul My lips are sealed.

Annie (*coyly*) Paul, can I ask you a personal question?

Paul Go right ahead.

Annie Where do you get all your ideas from?

He laughs and that's a mistake. He sees she's hurt and angry

Paul No, no, it's just that's the question everyone always asks writers— "where do all your ideas"——

Annie Well, if it's so dumb you get asked it all the time, then I expect you have a pretty special answer.

Paul I didn't mean it like that——

Annie No, go right ahead, Paul. I'm all ears. Where *do* you get all your ideas from?

Paul Well, all kinds of places—you know, things you hear, conversations, other books——

Annie No, *stupid*! I mean your *special* ideas. The ones that make the books come alive.

Paul I don't know, they just somehow——

Annie *Where do you get all your ideas from!*

Paul Nowhere. Nowhere!

Any other time and he would be punished. But not today. She turns back to the book and hugs it again

Annie I won't sleep tonight, Paul. I won't sleep a wink until I've finished this. Reading one of your books is like … being in love. No. It's better.

Fade to darkness

14   Misery

SCENE 6

The same. Night

Outside, the snow is falling. The Lights come up on the hall and Paul's room

Annie is reading his book, sitting in the hall. She is actually moving her head as she scans the page, lost in the story, wincing as though what she is reading is actually happening to her. She has a packet of biscuits beside her and she is cramming them in her mouth without even being aware of it. She drinks straight from a carton of chocolate milk

The TV is on low upstairs on the home shopping channel again. She's forgotten about it

Paul is fast asleep in the bedroom

We just hold on this scene for a few moments. Music and sounds from the old farmhouse

Fade to darkness

After a pause, the Light comes up slowly on Annie, who is still sitting in exactly the same place, now surrounded by various empty snack packets. She has been reading all night and she is now on the very last page of the book. She suddenly begins to inhale like an asthmatic. Something's wrong. She slaps her hand over her mouth like she's been stung. She begins to twist and turn the book in fury, as if she's unconsciously trying to tear the whole book in half

Annie No… (*She gets up and storms through the corridor straight into Paul's bedroom*) No!

He awakens with a start

Paul What? Annie? What is it? Are you all right?

She is not all right. She is almost speechless with rage

Annie You … you… *You dirty bird!*
Paul What's wrong? What have I done?
Annie She can't be dead! Misery Chastain cannot be dead!
Paul Annie, Annie, please——

Act I, Scene 6   15

She throws the book at the wall behind him, as hard as she can

Annie *Dirty bird! Oh, you dirty birdie! How could you?*
Paul She died giving birth! That often happened in those days! It—it—was a noble sacrifice, she gave her own life for her baby! And Misery's spirit will never die——
Annie I don't want her spirit! I want her! You killed her! You murdered her! (*She punches the bed in fury, just missing him*)
Paul I didn't!

She looks at him sarcastically

Annie Of *course* not. And if you didn't, Mr Paul Sheldon, then who did?
Paul No-one! (*He pauses*) She just ... died.
Annie I thought you were good, but you're not good. You're just a lying old dirty birdie.
Paul Annie, she ... she slipped away, that's all. It was like life, when someone just——
Annie People in stories don't just "slip away"! You're in charge, you're God, you make everything happen! Oh boy, you must think I was born yesterday! I was a nurse! I know how people die! I had dozens of people die in my own arms, I... (*She blanks out again. For a long time. Stands looking at the wall. She looks completely crazy. Eventually she comes back and looks down at him and speaks really quietly*) I think I better go now. I don't think I better be around you for a while. I don't think that's wise.
Paul Go? Where?
Annie A place I know. If I stay here I'll do something unwise. Goodbye, Paul. (*She goes to the door*)

Paul watches her, alarmed

Paul Will you be back to give me my medication?

She shuts the door without answering. She goes down the hall like a robot, picking up her parka and the ring of keys hanging up by the door

Annie leaves, double locking the front door

As the Lights start to dim, we hear footsteps in the snow, and the car driving off

16   Misery

SCENE 7

The same

Complete darkness

Paul I really need my Novril. Annie? I'm going to scream out loud if I don't get my Novril.

The following should occur in a deliberately dream-like way, with constantly shifting music and lighting, to convey Paul's delirious state as he is left alone for two days

I know you're there. So you can come out and stop playing games.

Darkness

(*Shouting at the top of his lungs*) HELP ME! OH, PLEASE SOMEONE HELP ME!!

There is no answer, of course

Dim light comes up on Paul's room. He has wrapped all the sheets around himself in a twisted knot. He's very agitated

You're in trouble. You're in deep shit. But you're going to get out. You're going to get out. Come on. Sooner or later somebody's going to come around here. The Roydmans ... someone. (*He reaches out and picks up an already empty glass on the dresser. He turns it upside down above his mouth and sucks and sucks at it, hoping to discover a drop of water he has missed*)

Darkness

(*Laughing*) She's probably had a crash. She's had a car crash, I'm just going to die here, of hunger ... or thirst ... or just *pain*! Some fucking horse race that'll be. Seven to five on Novril Boy. (*He's talking to himself in the darkness and he sounds like he's losing his sanity*) Annie, are you out there? Are you outside the door now, damn you?! You've made me a junkie with this morphine or codeine or whatever shitload of elephant dope it is ... you could at least give me my fix, you bitch!

Dim light

Act I, Scene 8

17

He makes a superhuman effort to try and move, gritting his teeth against the savage pain. When he finally gives up, he lets out a strangled sob, and then succumbs to crying

The Lights fade up and down continuously. Paul bangs his head back on the pillow, again and again, as he talks madly

They must have found your car by now. There'll be news stories and everything. "Found a wrecked car halfway down humbuggy mountain— Mmmm! Must belong to that famous Paul Sheldon, he must have crawled off in a daze—you know what these creative types are like!"

The light is going as he gets weaker

I need water and food and my Novril! I need them, Annie! (*He sobs*) I need them! I don't want to die here!

Darker

Well, Paul. You always wanted to know what it was like to drink your own piss...

Darkness

SCENE 8

The same. Two days later

Out of the darkness comes glorious, blinding daylight

Annie is standing over Paul, smiling and full of life. She holds a glass of water

Annie I have a cool, fresh glass of water for you. (*She smiles*) No, I'm not a mirage.

Paul forces himself to sit up, wincing in agony. He takes a gulp and she has to snatch it back from him

A little at a time or you'll vomit. (*She gives it back*)

He takes a small sip

18   Misery

Paul The capsules. The pain, please, Annie, please, for God's sake help me, the pain is so bad!

Annie I know it is, but I had to get away and think. My thoughts are often … muddy, I know that. So I prayed. I said "Dear God, Paul Sheldon may be dead when I get back". But God said "No, I have spared him so you can show him the way he must go". (*She produces some Novril and puts them down on the other side of the room, cruelly out of reach*) I will give you the medication. But first you have a little job to do. (*She goes out of the room*)

Paul Annie, don't torment me! Treat me like a human being! I'm in terrible pain!

Annie I know my dear. Soon.

Paul hears a clattering noise and Annie enters, wheeling an old metal barbecue into the room. She places it in the corner, where he can see it clearly. Paul looks perplexed. Annie suddenly opens the doors of the barbecue as though she's revealing a wonderful roast

Ta da!

On the grill pan is a stack of scrunched-up pages, a funeral pyre of typed pages, and Paul suddenly recognizes it

Fast Cars.

Paul Oh, no, no, Annie, that's the best thing I've ever done.

Annie I beg to differ. (*She picks up a box of matches and rattles it*)

Paul Burn it! Go on. (*He laughs*) Burn it. You think I haven't bothered to make a copy?

Annie just smiles

You know how much I get for writing a book, Annie? You think that's the only copy?

Annie Yes, Paul. I think it's the only copy.

Paul (*after a pause*) Please.

Annie It's disgusting. That aside, it's also no good.

Paul You wouldn't know good if it walked up and spat in your face!

Annie First of all, good would *not* spit in my face. Evil might, but not good. Second of all, I *do* know good when I see it. *You're* good, Paul. All you need is help. (*She holds out the matches to him*)

Paul For Chrissake!

Annie Use all the profanity you want. I've heard it all before.

Paul No. I won't do it. No. (*He turns away and closes his eyes*)

She starts rattling the bottle of pills

Act I, Scene 8 19

Annie When you burn it, *then* I'll give you the capsules. A double dose because it's been so long. All the pain will vanish. You'll begin to feel … serene. And I'll change your bedding—I see you've wet it, and it must be uncomfortable. I'll also change you. And by then you'll probably be hungry——

Paul I am hungry! I'm starving!

Annie —and I'll give you some soup. Some thick buttery toast. But until you burn that book, Paul, I can do nothing.

He rolls away from her

Paul I hate you.

She smiles

Annie Oh yes! That's what a child says. He says "Mommy, I hate you! You're mean!" The mother feels bad but she knows she's right, and she does her duty. As I am doing mine. (*She waits*) Well, Paul?

Paul No!

Annie It's with the trash, Paul, because that's where it belongs.

He's near to sobbing now

I can come back tomorrow if you like. Although I rather suspect you may go into a coma before too long.

Paul No!

Annie Well, you are a stubborn little boy. I'll drop by tomorrow and see if you've changed your——

Paul All right! (*Despising himself*) All right. Burn it, then.

Annie Oh, no. *I* can't do it, much as I'd like to spare you the agony.

Paul Why not? Why ever not?!

Annie Because you must do it of your own free will.

Paul laughs then, he can't help himself, and Annie looks very angry. She takes the title page from the top of the pile and holds it out, jamming it in his face

Paul Why are you making me do this!?

Annie I'm not making you do anything. It's your own free will.

Finally Paul opens the box of matches. He lights one. He moves it underneath the page and holds it there until it catches light

Good boy. (*She places it in the barbecue carefully so that it will set light to the other pages*) Good boy. (*As it burns, she stares at it, like a child who*

20   Misery

has accidently set a fire, a mixture of fear and excitement) Goodness! Oh
boy!

*Paul's masterpiece burns up in front of his eyes. Annie checks that everything
is burning smoothly, then she gives him his tablets*

Slow fade to darkness

Scene 9

The same. Very early Christmas morning

*Christmas carols. Tiny lights come up on a silver Christmas tree in Paul's
room. Around it are several presents, all wrapped. It's still dark outside*

Annie's standing above his bed

Paul (*sleepily*) What *time* is it?

She suddenly blows a cracker whistle in Paul's face

Annie It's five thirty.
Paul In the morning?!

*Now she's off and rooting around the bottom of the Christmas tree like a pig
looking for truffles, feeling the packages*

Annie I know it's early, but it's Christmas and I just couldn't wait. This is
so exciting! Paul! Look! Oh, what's this? (*She picks up a present wrapped
in cheap, gaudy paper and reads the tag*)
Paul To Annie ... with special love from Paul!

She turns to him with that same sly look in her eyes

Annie I knew you couldn't really get me anything, but that doesn't matter.
We'll pretend. (*She laughs*) So what have you got me?
Paul (*shrugging*) It's a surprise. I just hope you like it.

*She opens the wrapping paper to reveal a tin "smoker"—a little can with a
nozzle and a small bellows attached, for subduing bees with smoke*

Annie Why Paul, it's a new smoker for my bees! You must have known my

Act I, Scene 9

old one was coming to pieces! You *are* thoughtful. It's beautiful. You are so good. (*She kisses him on the cheek*) A present deserves a present in return. This is your big present. I put it in here last night while you were asleep. (*She drags out something huge from behind the tree*) "To Paul. Festive greetings and love from Annie."

It's a wheelchair. The chair part has been ridiculously wrapped in Christmas paper and there is a bow on the backrest. She puts it right by his bed

We need you mobile now you're getting better, don't we!
Paul (*nervously*) Yeah, sure. What for, particularly?
Annie So you can sit up at the table, dummy. Because what else is there under the tree?! Oh my! What could this be?! It's certainly heavy enough! (*She lifts a wrapped present the size of two telephone directories and puts it down beside Paul*) Have you guessed? Do you know what it is?

He shakes his head and reads the tag

Paul "To the greatest writer in the World, from his Number One Fan."
Annie That's me! Open it.
Paul OK. (*He opens the package to reveal an old ugly black typewriter*)

She beams

It's a Royal... God, it's a real antique!

Her smile disappears

Annie I know it's secondhand. But it's *good* secondhand!
Paul (*quickly*) I didn't mean anything—hey a good typewriter lasts forever. It's great.
Annie I got it at Pen To Paper. Isn't that a stupid name for a store? But Nancy Dartmonger, who runs it, is a very stupid woman. Dartmonger! Her name ought to be Whoremonger. Divorced twice and now she's living with a bartender. That's why when you said it looks like an antique——
Paul No, it looks fine. Really. I love it.
Annie She wanted forty-five dollars but she gave me five off because of the missing N. See? There's no N—it's missing one of its teeth. (*She tilts it up*)
Paul (*completely insincerely*) What does that matter?
Annie I told her N was an important letter. It's one of the letters in my favourite writer's name.
Paul It's two of the letters in my favourite nurse's name.
Annie (*embarrassed*) You fooler!

22   Misery

He gives her a big, fat, fake smile

Paul Annie, I've heard the TV up in your bedroom ... gosh, I really miss
keeping in touch with what's going on in the world and everything. I don't
suppose, as it's Christmas, you could bring it down here today and——
Annie Not without breaking my back, I couldn't, Paul! (*She laughs*) It's not
exactly a portable!
Paul Right. I was just wondering if there had been anything on the local news
about my disappearance? I mean it seems so strange, all these weeks, and
no-one's come looking for me... They haven't, have they?

Annie says nothing

Maybe another phone call would——
Annie Paul, I'm getting really sick and tired of this. I *told* you, I rang your
agent's office and I left this number, and if she doesn't want to call you back
then that's not my problem, is it?
Paul No, but maybe another——
Annie Well, is it *my* problem?!
Paul (*after a pause*) I guess not.
Annie Thank you. Boy, we haven't finished with your presents! I've got you
some writing paper! Oh—now I've spoilt the surprise—never mind! Open
it! (*She picks up another present*)

He starts to peel off the paper

I'll set everything up and we'll have a regular little writer's den. Well?
Well?
Paul Great. What will I write, do you think?
Annie Oh, but Paul, I don't think, I know! You're going to write a new novel!
Your best novel! *Misery's Return*!

He looks at her in disbelief

It'll be my reward for nursing you back to health! And you can start today!
Paul But Annie, it's Christmas Day. You were going to bring the TV down
and we were going to play cards and everything. Weren't we?
Annie Do you know how much I've spent on your Christmas?
Paul Look, Misery is dead. I'm sorry but that's——
Annie Even when I was mad at you, I knew she wasn't really dead.
(*Dreamily*) You couldn't really kill her, because you're good. In fact,
we're going to find out just how good you are, Mister Man! We'll set up
your new typewriter at the table and——
Paul I don't know if I can even sit in that wheelchair——

Act I, Scene 9 23

Annie Well, let's see, shall we?
Paul I don't know—I'm pretty heavy——

She leans over and grabs him under the arms, locking her arms around his back

Annie Don't be a baby. You think this is the first time I've put a man in a wheelchair?!

It is agony for him. He grits his teeth as she lifts him across and then lowers him into the chair

Yes! I know it hurts! It *will* hurt. Maybe an awful lot to start with. But there'll come a day soon when it'll hurt a little less. And a little less.

He tries to get comfortable as she arranges his pinned legs so they look right

Good as new, almost. And now you've got your mobility I know you won't abuse my trust.
Paul No, of course not. (*He finally settles, but it's obviously very painful*) Annie, will you promise me one thing?
Annie Of course.
Paul If I write this story for you——
Annie Novel! A great big one like the others. Maybe even bigger!

He takes this in for a moment

Paul OK, if I write this novel for you, will you let me go when it's done?

She looks at him uneasily

Annie You talk like I'm keeping you prisoner.

He says nothing. She waits for him to reply. To deny the accusation. He does not

(*Begrudgingly*) I guess that by the time you finish, you should be up to the ... the strain of meeting people again. Is that what you wanted to hear?
Paul That's what I wanted to hear.
Annie Well, honestly! I knew writers were supposed to have big egos, but I didn't realize how ungrateful they were!
Paul I'll need all the other books, if you've got them, so I can cross check dates and things——
Annie If I've got them? Are you joking? Oh, I'm going to bind *Misery's*

24   Misery

Return myself. A hardback. (*She grins*) There's lots of candy in your stocking, but don't fill up because in a couple of hours I'll be in with the biggest turkey dinner you ever saw, with bacon and sugared potatoes, and sweet apple sauce and peas cooked in orange juice! It's already sizzling away!

Paul Annie, in two hours it'll be eight o'clock in the morning.

Annie You'll be hungry when you smell it! And I've got pumpkin pie with strawberry ice cream because you've been such a good boy! You can even have an extra Christmas pill if you need it. Because you have to be strong to work. You'll mend faster when you're working, I'll bet! I'll go out now so you can put on your thinking cap. This is so exciting. Don't you think so? (*She goes to the door, hovers, and grotesquely blows him a kiss*)

Paul Annie—I'm afraid I can't start today.

Annie (*after a pause*) Oh?

He lifts the packet of paper, still half-wrapped in gift paper

Paul This paper's no good.

Annie But it's the most expensive… Nancy said so in Pen To Paper!

Paul Didn't your mother ever tell you that the most expensive is not always the best?

Annie No, she did *not*. What she told me, Mr Smart Guy, is that when you buy cheap you get cheap. (*She is starting to breathe more rapidly, almost to hyperventilate, clenching and unclenching her fists*)

He tries to tough it out

Paul And you might as well stop that. Getting mad won't change the paper.

She freezes as if he's slapped her

Annie You're trying to trick me because you don't want to write my book. I knew you would. Oh boy.

Paul If you give me a pencil I'll show you what the problem is.

She brings one over and slams it down on the dresser. It is all chewed and horrible

Watch. (*He removes a sheet from the pack. He takes the pencil and draws a line across the paper. Then he runs across it with his thumb*) You see how it smudges? Ribbon ink will do just the same thing——

Annie Oh, and you're going to sit and rub every page with your thumb, are you?

Paul When you're working, you're always hunting back to find a name, or

Act I, Scene 9

25

a date ... just the shift of the pages will blur everything. Editors hate Corrasable paper—it's one of the first things you learn in this business.

Annie Don't call it that!

Paul What?

Annie A business. Your talent is a gift from God.

Paul Sorry.

Annie You *ought* to be. You might as well call yourself a whore.

Paul (*restraining himself*) A good point. Now, getting back to the paper——

Annie I'll get your cockadoodie paper. Just tell me what to get.

Paul We want it to look good for the publisher——

Annie *I told you! I'm binding it myself!*

Paul Annie, I'm on your side——

Annie Don't make me laugh. No-one's been on my side since my mother died.

Paul A book should last a lifetime, Annie, and if I write on this paper——

Annie (*coldly*) You don't have to talk any more. What kind?

Paul Ask for a ream of long grain mimeo. Hammermill Bond is good, or Triad Modern. It'll cost much less and——

She gets up suddenly

Annie I'll go right now.

Paul (*quickly*) You don't have to do that. The Corrasable is fine to start with, after all, I'll have to rewrite anyway——

Annie Oh no, Paul, only an idiot would start good work with a bad tool.

Paul But it's Christmas—the store will be closed——

She takes the smudged sheet and screws it up into a ball with real violence

Annie Nancy lives above the store. I'll get her to open up, especially for you. I'm sure she won't mind a bit, even if she's in the middle of cooking her Christmas dinner for all her family and all her relatives because nothing is too much trouble for you Paul, *nothing!* I know you want to get started just as soon as you can since you're on my side, so I'm not even going to take time to put you back to bed or give you your pills. (*She picks up the paper and goes to the door*)

Paul Annie, really, I can start if you'll just——

Annie I know I look slow and stupid. But I am not stupid, Paul, and I am certainly not slow. (*Suddenly she rushes back across the room with the paper and brings it smashing down on his knees*)

Paul screams like he's never screamed in the whole of his adult life—pain like this is unimaginable

26   Misery

You sit there and you scream if you want to, because no-one can hear you. (*She walks to the door and then turns again*)

He screams in anticipation, which only makes her grin more widely

Nobody stops here because they all know Annie Wilkes is crazy. They think I got away with it, and they're right. Think about that, Paul, while I'm in town getting your cockadoodie paper. And if your turkey's black as tar you'll still eat every last piece, even if I have to shove it down your throat. You've spoilt Christmas.

Annie leaves, slamming the front door

Paul hears the clicks as she locks it. He tries to hold his legs, but he can't even touch them, it's so painful—it's like they're horribly burnt

Paul Please God ... get me out of this——

He hears another door slam and the car start up and drive away. He leans back in his chair, shaking all over. He puts his head in his hands

Come on, Paul. Come on. She's crazy ... she's going to kill you... Come on. (*He grits his teeth and grabs the wheels, pushes himself forward towards the door, crying out at the effort of moving himself with hands that have grown weak. He gives up after two pushes*) Come on. You're one phone call away from getting out of here. (*He starts up again, and steers the wheelchair—just—through the doorway and into the hall. He is in great pain*) I just *cannot* believe the guts of this Sheldon kid today... Nobody in the Annie Wilkes stadium believed he had a *chance* of getting that old wheelchair going after the blow he took, but yes! Look at him go! Sheldon's going for gold in the Special Olympics. (*He sees a black telephone at the far end of the hall. He wheels himself slowly down the hall and finally lifts the phone. He listens*) Shit. (*He pulls at the lead, expecting it to come away in his hand, but it's securely plugged into the wall socket. Then he slowly turns the whole phone upside down and sees there are no insides*) Good thinking, Annie—no insides—no nasty bills to pay!

He starts to turn the chair around and suddenly freezes: a car is approaching

She's coming back, she's coming back! (*He starts to shake—he'll never get back to his room in time*)

He listens in horror as the car gets louder and louder—and then passes without stopping

Act I, Scene 10 27

Take that as a warning. Get back in bed. (*He sets off again. Each movement is a marathon*) Just as soon as we've had a little Novril-burger, to dull the pain! Where's my Novril, Annie? Come on, be a sport. Where do you keep them? (*He pushes open another door in the hall and wheels down to the bathroom. He's panting like he's run up a mountain. Once inside, he pulls on the dangling light switch, illuminating the room with a naked bulb*) Jesus... You little squirrel...

The tiny room is piled high with stolen drugs; it looks like a mini-pharmacy

Where are they, then? Where do you keep Paulie's Novril? (*He scans the shelves—then he sees them: just out of reach. He braces himself by gripping one side of the chair with his left hand, then tries to push his whole body up so he can reach them with his other hand. The shelf is at full stretch and his left hand is shaking wildly as he tries to hold his weight. He is almost crying with the pain. He gets a finger to the packets, then he collapses back into his chair and clutches his knees, face contorted*) I need my pills! (*He tries again, straining in agony as he half-stands out of the chair, grinding his teeth in pain. As he finally reaches the Novril, closing his fingers around the bottle—he blacks out*)

We slowly fade out, with Paul slumped unconscious in his wheelchair

Scene 10

The same. Later that morning

The Lights come up on the hall, bathroom and Paul's room

Paul is asleep in the bathroom

In the distance we hear the four wheel drive coming back. We hear it stop, then the footsteps in the snow, approaching the door. Keys go into two locks

Paul suddenly jerks awake like somebody's put fifty thousand volts through him. For a few seconds he is completely paralysed with fear

Annie comes in the door, carrying his paper

Annie I've got your paper. Boy, I hope you appreciate all the trouble you've put me through. (*She takes off her coat and hangs it in the hall, then slips off her boots*)

28   Misery

*Paul reaches up and yanks the light switch off as Annie walks back down the
hall. She goes towards his room but then she walks upstairs instead*

(*Going upstairs*) Nancy was still wallowing in bed, but that's not surprising,
I didn't exactly think she'd be on her knees in church.

Annie disappears upstairs

*Paul frantically wheels back through the hall, pulling the bathroom door shut
behind him*

(*Off*) I had to hammer on the door for about five minutes before she came
down—half-dressed and probably half-drunk. She was effing and blinding
and telling me I was crazy but she opened the store eventually. That whore
would open her mother's coffin for five dollars.

*Paul wheels backwards down the hall and into his room, pushing the door
shut as——*

Annie comes back down, now wearing her slippers

Paul? Have you gone back to sleep? I hope that turkey's all right for your
sake, 'cause you're going to eat it even if it isn't.

Annie enters his room as Paul is still backing away from the door

This had better be the right pape—— (*She suddenly breaks off, frowning*)
You're *dripping* with sweat… What have you been doing?

Paul doesn't know what to say. He's out of breath

Answer me! What have you been doing!?

Long pause

Paul I… I… I've been suffering. As you well know…

She takes out a handkerchief and wipes his brow

Annie Has it been very bad?
Paul I tried to get back in bed but I couldn't. This chair really hurts…
Annie Well, I told you about making me mad. Live and learn, isn't that what
they say? Well, if you live I guess you'll learn.

Act I, Scene 10   29

Paul Can … can I have my pills now?

Annie In a minute. First I want to make sure there's nothing else stupid old Nurse Wilkes forgot because she doesn't know how a smart guy goes about writing a book. I want to make sure you don't want me to go back into town and get you a special novel writer's tape recorder, or maybe a pair of writing slippers, or something like that. Because if you want me to, I'll go. Your wish is my command. I won't even wait to give you your pills. I'll hop right into old Bessie again and go. So what do you say, Mister Smart Guy? You all set?

Paul I'm all set. Annie, please——

Annie And you won't make me mad any more?

Paul No, I won't make you mad any more.

Then she looks down at his hands

Annie Paul, why are you holding your hands like that?

He looks down and realises he's still clutching the Novril bottle, covering it with his hands. He begins to cry

I asked you a question.

Paul I… I want my urinal. I held it all the time you were gone, Annie, but I can't any longer and I don't want to wet myself again.

Annie You poor dear. Annie's put you through a lot, hasn't she? Too much! Mean old Annie! I'll get it right away. And your pills.

As soon as she goes out, he wheels back and stuffs the pills under the mattress, then wheels back as Annie returns with the urinal and his Novril. He greedily swallows the pills. She holds out the urinal

Do you need help?

Paul I can do it. (*He half-turns the chair away from her. He takes the glass urinal*)

She pretends to look away. Next door, Jingle Bells *starts up on the radio. She stands there, smiling as he urinates*

The Lights dim slowly

Curtain

ACT II

Spring

SCENE 1

The farmhouse. Day

The Lights come up on Paul's room. It's the beginning of spring. All the snow has gone, and we can see the farmhouse more clearly

With the snow gone, the tree outside Paul's window looks like half-house, half-tree. Hanging in the tree is a large, sticky beehive

Annie has moved Paul's bed, and brought in a table for him to work at, by the window. Unfortunately it is positioned so the door is behind it, and he cannot see when she enters the room in her silent nurse's manner

Paul is much stronger now, and moves more easily. He is in his wheelchair, holding a small sheaf of papers, and facing a very excited Annie

Paul (*reading*) "*Misery's Return*. Chapter One: Rebirth. (*Beat*) Rory Carmichael burst into the huge kitchen of his manor house on the banks of Loch Dunthorpe, announcing his homecoming by hurling a brace of pheasants on to the ancient kitchen table. (*Beat*) He ripped off his soaking shirt and let it drop carelessly on the floor, running his strong fingers through his sopping blond hair. He could hear the strains of Chopin from the great hall beyond, and suddenly the moisture running down his masculine cheeks was not rainwater, but tears, as the memory of Misery's desperate dance with the Grim Reaper overwhelmed him. (*Beat*) Her labour had been long and brutal, but it was only when the midwife had urged Rory to ride for the doctor that he had realized his darling wife was near death. Her terrible screaming would be forever etched on his heart. (*Beat*) As Rory now strode manfully towards the great hall, he gave silent thanks for the healthy cry of his son upstairs, and he smiled to himself as he heard the comforting lullaby sung by Annabel Wilkes, surely the best children's nurse in the whole of Scotland."

Annie squirms with embarrassment and pride

Act II, Scene 1 31

"As Rory entered the great hall, Misery arose from behind the grand piano and breathlessly rushed into his arms. (*Beat*) Rory held her like a precious jewel, her chestnut hair cascading over him in gorgeous profusion. He simply couldn't bare to contemplate what life would be like if he had arrived with the doctor even five minutes later on that terrible night two months ago, or if the experimental blood transfusion had not worked, in which he had so bravely sliced opened his forearm and poured his life's blood into Misery's depleted veins. (*Beat*) 'My darling,' said Misery, and——"

Annie Stop, Paul.

Paul puts the pages down

Paul What's wrong?
Annie I think you know what's wrong.
Paul Don't you like it? It's——
Annie It's a cheat. Oh, it's beautiful, Paul. But it's still a dirty cheat.
Paul (*flabbergasted*) Why!?

Annie grabs the pages from him

Annie Rory rode for the doctor at the end of *Misery's Child*. That bit's right. But the doctor never came, because Rory's horse tripped on that rotten Mr Griggor's toll gate, and Rory broke his ribs and lay there all night in the rain. So the doctor *never* came. You see?
Paul No, I don't see! It's Misery, just like you asked me for...
Annie Oh boy, you must think I'm awful stupid!
Paul I don't, I don't——
Annie When I was a girl, I used to go to the movies every Saturday. What I liked best was the Chapter plays. Rocket Man was my favourite. Each week it ended with him in terrible trouble—unconscious in a crashing plane, or tied to a chair in a burning warehouse, or about to get fried with ten thousand volts shoved through him... (*She's getting herself worked up again*) And then it stopped, and you spent the whole week wondering how he'd get out. Like when he was unconscious in the airplane. He came around and found a parachute under his seat, and jumped out, and that was fair enough.

Paul can't help laughing, and when she looks sharply at him he quickly converts it into a coughing fit. She thumps him on the back hard enough to hurt

Better?

32   Misery

Paul Yes, thanks.
Annie Can I go on now, Paul, or were you planning to have a sneezing fit? Should I get the bucket? Do you think you might have to vomit a few times?
Paul No, Annie. Please go on.

She stares at him for a moment

Annie When he found the parachute, well, maybe it wasn't realistic, but it was *fair*. But then there was this episode where the bad guys put Rocket Man in a car with no brakes, and welded all the doors shut, and pushed him down a twisty mountain road ending in this huge cliff! And there was poor old Rocket Man, trying to stop the car, *and* steer, *and* open the door all at the same time, and then … then the car went over the cliff and—and hit the rocks and burst into flames and went into the ocean! (*She sits on the bed, hands tightly clasped together*) Oh boy, I was on the edge of my seat, I can tell you! The next week I was waiting outside the theatre two hours before it opened. The episode always started with the end of the last one. Rocket Man was racing down the hill like before, banging on the door, trying to open it. Then, just before the car got to the edge, the door opened and he rolled out on to the road! (*She stops mid-story, as astonished now as the first time she saw it*) And all the kids in the theatre cheered, but not me! I was mad! That isn't what happened last week! That isn't what happened! (*She begins to walk backwards and forwards, twisting Paul's first chapter*) Are you all too stupid to remember!? Did you all get amnesia? That was a dirty cheat!! (*She looks at him murderously*) He didn't *get* out of the cockadoodie car! It went over the edge and he was still inside! Do you understand?
Paul Yes.

She rips up all his work in front of his face

Annie *Do you understand that?!*
Paul Yes, Annie, yes!

She throws the pieces contemptuously on the bed

Annie Then you know what's wrong.
Paul I suppose I do.
Annie Then you'd better fix it. And you'd better fix it by tomorrow night, because I've had enough of all your excuses.

Black-out

Act II, Scene 3   33

SCENE 2

The same. Day

Before the Lights come up on Paul's room, we hear something that sounds like a gun shot. Then another. Then several in rapid succession. A machine gun scatter and then the sound changes and we finally recognize it as rapid typing

Paul is trying to work at his desk. He suddenly stops, looks at what he's written and shakes his head

Paul Come on, get inspired. Get fucking inspired! (*After checking she's not around, he opens his secret bottle of pills and swallows some tablets*) You've got to cut down on all the dope you're taking, Paul, or you'll give yourself a bad habit. (*He laughs*) A worse habit, you junkie. Only not today. Let's wait until you get a chapter your Number One Critic actually likes. You thought *Fast Cars* was good, Paul? It was cockadoodie! (*He pulls the page out of the typewriter and takes a pencil to it, filling in the gaps with Ns*) Rory had (*he writes*) N-ever really accepted that Misery was dead, (*he writes*) N-or forgiven himself for (*he writes*) N-ot... (*He suddenly screws it up and throws it at the wastebin*) Shit. Shit! (*He carefully threads a new piece of paper into the machine*) OK. OK. What we've got here is lots of talk and white space.

He starts typing again, the sound of his typing getting louder and louder, as the Lights fade slowly to Black-out

SCENE 3

Paul's room. Night

Outside it's a windy night, and we can hear creaking and noises from the house and the other farm buildings

Paul is sitting up in bed, looking nervous. Annie is sitting in a chair, eating honey from a jar, dipping a knife in and licking it clean

Paul "*Misery's Return*, by Paul Sheldon. Chapter One: Voices From The Grave. (*Beat*) For a moment Rory was not sure who the trembling figure in the darkness was. 'Oh Sir, please forgive me disturbing ye at this late hour, but I couldnae sleep!' It was only when the terrified old man shuffled into the light of the doorway that Rory recognized him as Smeggs, the

34   Misery

village gravedigger. Only three days previously, Rory had watched Smeggs shovel wet earth on poor Misery's coffin after the heartbreaking funeral service. (*Beat*) 'It's the noises in the churchyard, sir. Horrible scratching sounds... Her Ladyship rests not easy!'"

The wind outside becomes subtly mixed with other sounds from the story— a barn owl... nails scratching wood... Annie has stopped eating

"Rory despatched Smeggs back into the night, telling him not to be so stupid. But less than five minutes later, after almost gagging on a giant tumbler of malt, he had hitched up the horses and was riding the pony-trap through the dark night. (*Beat*) His ribs were still agony from where the doctor had taped them up after he fell from his horse— (*he looks at Annie sarcastically*) on that rotten Mr Griggor's toll gate..."

Now we can hear the sound of the pony and trap, again so subtle underneath the noise of the wind that we might almost be imagining it

"Smeggs' words alone would not have put Rory into his present state of terror. But when the local doctor had examined poor Misery's body, he had said something very queer: 'It's not a bit like Charlotte Evelyn-Hyde. I have satisfied myself of that'."
Annie Who's Charlotte Evelyn-Hyde? She's not in the other Misery books!
Paul Do you want me to read, or do you want to ask questions?
Annie No, sorry, Paul. Read on!

Paul knows she's hooked now. He makes a fuss of pretending to be angry before he settles down and we once again return to the world of the nineteenth century

Paul "Charlotte Evelyn-Hyde had been found dead in her back garden. The doctor had pronounced it to be a heart attack, although the girl was only eighteen. Four days after she was buried, the village prostitute, Miss Roydman, had staggered drunkenly through the graveyard and tripped over something white on the ground. She shrieked like a banshee when she realized it was a hand, the torn fingers thrusting up hideously through the earth of a fresh grave. Poor Charlotte had clearly fallen into some deathlike coma, only to wake and find herself buried alive. She had tried to dig herself out. As this awful memory came back to him, Rory jerked the horses to a halt outside the gates of the graveyard."

We hear the horses being pulled to a halt, footsteps racing across a gravel footpath, and the tolling of a church bell. Annie is now jigging in her chair like a kid who needs to go to the toilet

Act II, Scene 3 35

"He rushed to Misery's tombstone as the church clock hammered midnight. He threw himself on the ground and forced his ear against the earth."

Annie is beside herself with expectation: it is totally real for her

"For what seemed like an eternity he remained motionless, listening, and then suddenly he heard the sound of weak hands clawing at wood deep below, and he let out a single, breathless sob. 'Misery! Misery! I'm here! Hold on, my darling!'"

Paul puts down the pages and the wind outside dies down. Annie looks pale

Well? Is it fair?

Annie looks at him with fear and respect

Annie Oh yes, yes, it's fair! It's wonderful! But Paul, it's so gruesome! That poor woman who scraped the ends of her fingers off— (*She shakes her head*) It's not like the other Misery books.

Paul is intent on enjoying his single moment of power

Paul Well, I don't know, Annie. Maybe it's not right. Maybe I should tear it up?
Annie (*smiling*) I'll kill you if you do! I have to know what happens next! I want a new chapter every night ... like the cliff-hangers!
Paul I can't write a whole new chapter every day, Annie, that's too much work——
Annie You can! Like that girl who had to make up a new story each night for a thousand million nights!
Paul Scheherezade?
Annie And I can help, too! I'll fill in all the missing N's. I won't peek, I'll do it with my eyes squidged half-shut. Oh, read it again, Paul!
Paul I'm pretty tired now, if that's all right. I *have* been working all day and half of last night.
Annie Of course. I'll leave you alone. Oh Paul, I'm so excited! (*She goes to the door and then hovers. She looks very embarrassed*) Maybe it was a bee.
Paul What?
Annie That made it look like she was dead. She could have been stung by a bee, but everyone thought she died in childbirth! One person in twelve is allergic to bee-venom, and sometimes they cause a comatose state... In fact, a bee could have been why that other woman Charlotte was buried alive as well!

36   Misery

Paul laughs scornfully

Paul Oh yeah, two unrelated women in the same village are both buried alive
within six months because of bee stings?

Annie recoils at his sarcasm

Annie Well. You're the writer.
Paul Nice of you to say so.
Annie Paul, just forget I said anything.

And then suddenly... Suddenly it is the right idea

Paul No, wait a minute. They *could* be related! Yes! It would work if they
were related... Charlotte is really Misery's sister, or half-sister—that
would work better ... and the bees affected both of them *because* they're
both related!
Annie Did I help!? Did I?

He's already starting to go away into his own world

Paul Bring me a pencil. Maybe they've got the same hair or something ...
shit ... maybe someone else in the village *knows* that Misery was buried
alive! (*He starts scribbling notes, falling into his world*)

The Lights fade to Black-out

SCENE 4

The same. Day

Lights up on Paul's room

Outside it's pouring with rain; a dark, dull day

*The table lamp is on and Paul is typing fast at his desk, talking aloud his
thoughts as he writes them down*

*We hear the sounds of a large schooner at sea, and begin to see the outline
of the schooner's rigging, high in his room, moving as if in the wind*

Paul Throughout the voyage, Misery lay in her hammock, half-alive, half

Act II, Scene 4 37

dead, slipping into cataleptic trances at the slightest... No no no... (*He mumbles*) Rory knew that if she were ever to be stung by another bee—ever stung—good, yes ... ever to be stung she would die instantly... No no—she would ... she would... Misery would either be killed or cured instantly! (*He scans the page, makes faces and then accepts it. He starts typing again*)

Annie shuffles into the room behind him. Her hair is greasy and unwashed. She is wearing her housecoat and slippers, which are covered in food stains. There are marks on her arms and face and she is clutching something in her hand

The sounds fade

(*Still typing*) This is good, Annie, I'm cooking. I'll have a really special chapter for you tonight.

Annie Here. (*She throws his pills absent-mindedly at him*)

As the pills clatter on the desk, he looks up for the first time and immediately gets scared

Paul Annie? Are you all right?

Annie (*dreamily*) No.

Paul I've almost finished. I'm just re-writing the last bit. Would you like your story early today?

In reply she pulls out her lip and twists it hard, pinching it. He tries to ignore that

Sit down on the bed—go on. You remember how we left things last night?

She shakes her head slowly

Yes, you do. Rory and Misery boarded the *Lorelei*, the schooner for the trip——

Annie To the Dark Continent.

Paul Yeah, to Africa. Shall I read on?

Annie leans forward over his table lamp, wiping her mouth. Lit from underneath, she looks very sick

(*Reading*) Less than a hundred miles inland from Lawstown, the Dutch settlement on the northern tip of the Barbary Coast, lived the Bourkas, Africa's most feared native tribe, known as the Bee-People.

38   Misery

The sounds of an African port drift in

It took three days before Rory found a guide who would take them to Bourka country, a giant negro called Hezekiah who flashed seven gold teeth every time he smiled. He told——

Annie suddenly gets up

Annie? I'm not finished——

She stands in the corner of the room, her head pressed against the wall. Paul waits a second and then decides to carry on

He told fabulous tales of a huge woman's face carved in stone, jutting from the side of a crumbling cliff, a merciless face with a huge ruby set in her stone forehead.

Annie suddenly slaps herself around the face. Paul looks at her, horrified. She slaps herself again. Hard

Behind the idol's mouth was a honeycomb of caves——

Annie slaps herself again

—where a hive of giant albino bees lived...

Annie slaps herself. Paul gives up trying to read

Annie, you're very sick. I really think you should go into town and see a doctor.

Annie When I found it, it was still struggling. Now it's at peace. I guess. They come into the cellar when it rains. Poor things. (*She turns round and opens her hand. She's carrying a little rat in her hand, dangling from a small wooden trap. She drops it down into his lap, right on the page he is reading from*) I suppose you think of escaping. You can't. But we could both go together. (*She blanks out. Comes back*) I'm going into the shed to get my shotgun now, and I'm going to come back and put it in your mouth and pull the trigger. Then I'll turn it on myself. Maybe the next world's better than this one.

Paul No, Annie, you want me to finish the book, don't you?

He's never seen her like this. This bad

Annie Misery?

Act II, Scene 5

Paul Of course, Misery, yes! I agree the world is a pretty awful place, especially when it rains... I mean, I've been in a lot of pain these last weeks and——

Annie *Pain!?* You don't know what pain is. You haven't the slightest idea.

Paul No no, I suppose not. Not compared to you.

Annie That's right.

Paul But you want to know how the story turns out, don't you?

Annie That's the only thing in the whole world I still want. (*She goes to the door*) I have this place I go when I feel like this, in the hills. You remember Brer Rabbit telling Brer Fox about his Laughing Place? It has a wooden sign above the door which says "Annie's Laughing Place". I made it. Sometimes I do laugh when I go there. But mostly I just scream.

Black-out

The rain gets louder

SCENE 5

The same. Night

The Lights come up on Paul's room, the hall and kitchen

Paul is in his wheelchair, negotiating it through the bedroom doorway, then wheeling along the dark hall

Outside we can hear the pouring rain, and the thunder of a big storm. The farm animals are frightened

Paul wheels down the hall, past the door to the bathroom. There are no lights apart from the lightning, flashing on and off. As he reaches the bottom of the hall, he sees a small bookcase. There is a little light which he turns on

Paul Jesus...

The light illuminates a kind of weird shrine—all Paul's books, and above them dozens of faded magazine and newspaper cuttings stuck to the wall. In the centre is a big, glossy, signed photograph of Paul, in a horrible cheap frame. If it was once treasured, it has now been vandalised, and a fist-sized blow has shattered the glass, right through the middle of his face

(*Scared*) Your popularity is slipping, Paul. Number Two fan and falling.

40 Misery

He turns and looks back at the front door. He thinks about going back to his room—she could return at any minute. Then he decides to go on forward. He wheels around the corridor and into the tiny kitchen, every bit as filthy and neglected as the bathroom

Flashes of lightning illuminate the dark room. On and off, just like the light in the hall before. Sweet foods and unwashed plates are haphazardly stacked around the room. He goes to the back door, which has metal mesh to strengthen it. He tries the handle, shaking it violently before realizing there's no chance of getting out

I'm not going to give up. Come on, Paul! When she comes back she's going to kill you. (*He looks around the room for ideas*) Poison her. Enough Novril crunched up in her breakfast cereal and she'd go unconscious, and then... (*He shakes his head*) But she'd taste it, she's not stupid... (*He bangs the arms of the wheelchair in frustration*) You've got to get out of here before she gets back... Light a fire. Burn the place down, that'll bring somebody! But what if it takes too long? I'll end up like the Christmas turkey ... oh, fuck it. Fuck it fuck it fuck it! (*He sees the drawer by the cooker. He opens it and looks inside. Then he makes a momentous decision. Psyching himself up*) Do it. You have to do it. (*He takes out a huge kitchen knife*)

Massive thunder and lightning directly overhead

OK. When she comes back, you ask for a glass of water, because you're so thirsty... You're in bed because you're so weak, and then when she bends over and... (*He rehearses ramming the kitchen knife into her guts*) "It's the law of de jungle, Master Rory".

Another big flash of lightning and Black-out

SCENE 6

The same. Night

Silence except for a quiet trickle of water dripping off the roof. The storm is over

Paul is fast asleep in bed

A powerful flashlight suddenly comes on. Paul slowly wakes up

Act II, Scene 6   41

Annie has some kind of trolley at the bottom of his bed, and she has placed the flashlight on the top so it shines on Paul's face

Annie Did I ever tell you what lovely eyes you have? But I suppose other women have—women who were much prettier than me, and much bolder about their affections, as well. (*She rubs his arm with a cotton wool swab*)
Paul I was dreaming about Africa——

She suddenly injects him with a hypodermic

Annie, what are you doing!? What's happening?

Whatever it is, it's already rushing through Paul

(*Laughing*) Oh boy, whatever this stuff is, it's ... it's great... (*he laughs*) it makes that Novril look like...

The huge narcotic hits him properly

This is crystal top, oh God, this is ... this is walking on the clouds in a fucking Rolls Royce, this is...
Annie What do you want first, Paul? The good news or the bad news?
Paul Good news first. Guess you don't like the book much? Too bad, I tried...

She looks at him reproachfully

Annie I *love* the book, Paul. You *know* that.
Paul (*grinning like an idiot*) You love the book, so you can't be going to kill me ... so there can't be any bad news!... Oh boy, am I stoned!
Annie The good news is that your car is gone. I was very worried about it now the snow has melted. But the storms must have washed it into the river. It's gone ... poof! That's the good news. (*She rests her hand tenderly against his face*) Now that your car's gone it means you can really stay and finish my book. But do you *want* to stay? That's the question I have to ask myself, and much as I want to pull the wool over my eyes I know the answer to *that one*.

Paul says nothing. Annie suddenly moves off into the darkness, so he can hear her but not be exactly sure of where she is

When I was eleven my whole family were killed in a fire, all except me, Paul. Do you have any idea what that feels like?

Paul I guess not.

Annie You *guess* not. I've had more tragedy than one person can bear. They put me with a horrible mean family. It's not very Christian to say so, but I was glad when my stepfather died of food poisoning. When I was studying for my nursing exams my room-mate had what they called a freak fall. That was certainly the right word to describe her. Freak. She only fell one flight, but it was a stone floor. I called the hospital but…

Paul (*completely stoned*) Wow, look at the moonlight coming through the window.

Annie I got jobs in geriatric wards. St Joseph's. Riverview, and other places. (*She grimaces*) You have no idea of how … how *foul* old people can be, Paul. When they're sick, and nothing you do is right. A lot of them died. An awful lot.

Paul (*starting to slur*) I'm sorry, I'm drifting off——

Annie I preferred being a maternity nurse. And I was very good, *very good*, Paul, whatever they say. But there were more… (*sighs*) incidents and then would you believe it, they put me on trial for one of the babies who died. Some girl who wasn't even old enough to have a proper name. (*She's incredulous, even now, remembering it*) The press had a name for *me*, though, oh yes, they called me the Dragon Lady. The police had one hand mark on the girl's throat that was like mine, *like mine*, that was all! … and they also said I'd always been on duty when the deaths occurred. Well what does that prove? You tell me. What does that prove!?

Paul Nothing.

Annie *Nothing at all!* There were millions and billions of times when I was on duty and *nothing* happened!

Paul is struggling to stay conscious

Also, I don't believe babies are ensouled. Anyway, I was found innocent.

Paul Ah well, that's good.

Annie Everyone I ever love dies, Paul. It's as simple as that. (*She appears in the light again*) You know what kept me going, all the time I was sitting in that holding cell in Denver? Misery. I read all your books again, cover to cover. If it hadn't been for you I think I would have taken my own life, Paul. So when I found you in the snow … it wasn't a coincidence at all, was it? It was a real miracle.

Paul Best thing that ever happened to me. (*He laughs, completely stoned*)

Annie You remember when I went into town, because your writing paper wasn't *good* enough? That was when you went out the first time, wasn't it? And don't try and tell me you haven't been out, because all the hairs are broken.

Paul Hairs?

Act II, Scene 6

43

Annie You can use cotton, but I used hairs from my head. If they're broken you know someone's been snooping. Not that I was surprised. I knew you'd been out. I've known for a long, long time. That's the bad news.

Paul Oh.

Annie You wanted your pills. I should have known you'd do anything to get them, but when I get mad I get, you know ... oogy. I checked the bathroom and I thought some had gone, but I wasn't sure. How many times have you been out in all?

Paul Twice.

Annie Please tell the truth, Paul.

Paul Thassall, two times... Just to get water and (*he drifts*) and and pills...

Annie Oh, and you didn't try the telephone either time, I suppose, or look at the locks? Let me tell you, Paul, I've stretched strands of hair all over this house and they've *all* been snapped—in the hallway ... in my bedroom upstairs! In the shed outside!

Paul How could I get ... usstairs? (*He lurches forward, stoned, and tries to grab the knife he has hidden*)

She lets him fumble about for it

Annie Looking for this? (*She steps forward into the light again and holds up the gleaming kitchen knife*) I checked under the mattress before I gave you your pre-op anaesthetic. I expected to find capsules; the knife was a complete shock. I almost slit myself in two! But *you* didn't put it there, did you?

Paul What ... what do you mean ... anaesthetic?

Annie (*shouting*) Damn you! God damn you! How many times!? (*She throws a glass of water in his face to wake him up*) I say it was seven. At least seven. Was it seven?

Paul laughs

I can see you mean to be stubborn. I guess people like you get so used to lying for a living that you just can't stop doing it in real life. But that's all right. Because the *principle* doesn't change if you were out seven times, or seventy, or seventy times seven. The *principle* doesn't change, and neither does the *response*. (*She disappears into the darkness again*)

It's like a crazy, hallucinogenic dream—one minute she's there, the next she's gone, and Paul's stuck in a horrible state of semi-consciousness, head lolling one moment, jerking awake in stark terror the next

Have you ever read about the early days at the Kimberly diamond mines,

44

Paul? Sometimes the black workers stole diamonds. Poked them up their rectums. Do you know what you British did to them if they got caught?

Paul Killed them, I guessshh...

Annie Oh no! That's like junking an expensive car just because of a broken spring. They made sure that they could go on working ... but they also made sure they'd never run away again. The operation was called hobbling, Paul, and that's what I'm going to do to you. (*She rips the bedclothes right off, exposing his twisted legs*)

Adrenalin and fear wake him up and make him fight the drug

Paul No! No, Annie! Please...

But she has that slack, vacant look in her eyes. She bends down and picks up a small propane torch and puts it down on the dresser by the matches

What the fuck is that for!?

Annie I can't suture, there'll be no time. And a tourniquet's no good ... no central pressure point. I've got to cauterize.

She turns off the flashlight, leaving him in the pitch black. He hears her go to the door

Paul Annie! Annie, I'll stay right here! I won't ever get out of bed again! Please! Oh, please don't!

A stroboscope light starts flickering on and off as Annie comes straight back in, holding a massive, rusty axe

Annie Just a little pain, then this nasty business will be behind us.

Paul is screaming, trying to turn over, to turn away from her, to draw up his legs

Paul Annie, oh, Annie, please please, no, please, don't, Annie, I swear to you I'll be good, I'll be good, please give me a chance, I'll be good, I swear to God, oh Annie, please let me be good——

Annie Don't be a cry baby like the others. (*She grips the axe carefully and spreads her legs like a logger*)

The stroboscope light is blinking on and off with ever longer periods of darkness, so we are only seeing a flash for one second in every five

Paul Annie, *oh please please don't hurt me*!

Act II, Scene 7

Annie Keep still! I must do this properly!

The axe comes down into his leg on the Black-out

Screaming

Darkness

Screaming. Screaming

After ten seconds of darkness a second of illumination—now the bed and the axe are covered in blood and she's lifting it and swinging again

Darkness

Paul screams loud enough to crack the walls

Paul, for goodness sakes, I'm a trained nurse!

Screams and music

Screams in the darkness

Silence

After fifteen seconds of darkness a second of light

Just get rid of the trash. (*She picks up something that looks like a foot and drops it in the yellow floor bucket*)

Paul is beyond screaming. He's unconscious

Now you're hobbled and don't you blame me. Stay still while I cauterize.

Scene 7

The same

The sound of Chopin. Bees in the hive. Typing

We gradually fade up to see fresh flowers on the table in Paul's room. The music is coming from a radio on Paul's desk. It is a glorious day, and summer can't be far away. We can hear Annie a long way off, outside by the barn

46   Misery

Annie (*off*) Come on, Misery! Eat your feed! Pig! Pig! Pig!

As Paul types, he talks to himself, occasionally whistling a few bars of the music. His hair is wild, and he's wearing a stained T-shirt. If you saw him walking towards you on the street you'd cross over; he's grinning and he looks as crazy as she is

Paul Roll out those lazy, hazy crazy days of summer. You're doing well, Paul. In fact you're doing remarkably well for a man who couldn't write if he had a little headache or he didn't have a cigarette. Perhaps you should come to Annie's house every year to write. (*He moves his wheelchair to stretch*)

We see one foot is no longer there—just a slack trouser leg tied with string. He re-reads what he's written

Misery Misery Misery. *Misery's Return* will be available in a strictly limited edition of one, bound in the author's skin. (*He starts to type again and then curses. He carefully inserts his fingers like tweezers into the typewriter and pulls out a broken T hammer*) T! T ... T ... T! No N, and now no T! T—my God, it's the second most common letter in the English language! I'm going to complain to the management. I am not just going to ask for a new typewriter, I'm going to demand one.

Annie suddenly appears outside and grins through the window, gives him the thumbs up

Annie (*grinning*) I can't hear you working very hard!

He grins back at her and returns the gesture. She goes off again and he spies on her

Paul No. Better not to ask. Better not to provoke. Annie is not swayed by pleas or screams. She has the courage of her convictions. (*He slams the typewriter*) Go on and break, then. I'll finish anyway. I'll write longhand. I'll write on the back of my fucking hand if I need to. Because that's what I do. I go through the hole in the paper and I fly like a big dead bird all the way to Africa... (*He starts to type again*)

A slow, ominous jungle drum beat starts, steady and doom-laden, as the daylight starts to fade. His room is bathed in red light, the faint outline of a giant, hazy jungle sun on one side of the stage. Joining the drums comes the sound of bees

Act II, Scene 8   47

SCENE 8

The same. Night

While Paul reads, Annie is pacing the room, as though she wants to hear but she doesn't at the same time

Paul (*reading*) "'Let me go to her, I say!' Rory pulled backward with furious strength, and Hezekiah moaned fearfully 'No, boss, don't make dem bees crazy!' Rory's dress shirt, now torn in a dozen places, began to come apart as Hezekiah tried to restrain him. (*Beat*) 'Do you want to demonstrate your love by killing her, boss?' Hezekiah hissed. Rory ceased to fight, and instead looked again on the dreadful sight…'"

The bees get louder and more numerous, as though we're approaching a massive hive

"Misery had been tied to a post in a clearing, her slender arms and legs brutally spread-eagled and bound by jungle vines to two thick, wooden stakes. She wore not a stitch of clothing, yet Rory thought even the most prudish churchgoer could not have faulted her for indecency. Misery was far from naked. She was dressed in bees."

Annie is covering her ears, shaking her head

Annie You have to stop, Paul—— (*But she doesn't really want him to stop*)

The drums are pounding and the bee noise is a horrible, thick, heaving drone

Paul "Misery seemed almost to be wearing some strange nun's habit— strange because it moved and undulated constantly across the swell of her breasts and hips. (*Beat*) Now literally thousands of bees covered Misery in a thick and moving blanket."

Annie looks like she's going to die of anxiety. The bees and the drums

"Hezekiah whispered: 'As long as de drums beat, de bees will sleep, and she will live.' (*Beat*) 'But what if the drums stop?' Rory asked and just then, the drums did." (*He puts down the pages*)

The sounds stop and ordinary lighting returns

Annie How does she escape?! She has to escape!
Paul Maybe. Maybe not.

48   Misery

Annie I can't wait. Tell me the rest. Tell me how it ends.
Paul I can't do that. You wouldn't respect me in the morning.

She doesn't laugh

You'll have to wait.
Annie Well, I don't *want* to wait. Did Baron Heidzig betray Misery? That's
one thing I *really* want to know.

Paul shakes his head slowly in an I-won't-tell-anything manner

You're making me very angry—you know that, don't you?
Paul You remember telling me what the little kid says to his mother?
"Mommy, you're mean!" Isn't that what you're saying? "Paul, you're
mean!"
Annie Whoo boy, gosh, if you make me much madder, I won't be
responsible. I could make you *tell*.
Paul If I give you what you want, you won't want it any more.

She stares at him with pure malice

Annie You know what I think? I think you're *never* going to finish. I think
you're wilfully slowing down so you won't *ever* finish!
Paul Annie, what do you want?! I've written you a whole new chapter every
single day!
Annie Short chapters!
Paul I can't go any faster!
Annie Well, at least tell me if that nigger Hezekiah knows where Misery's
father is! Tell me that!
Paul You want me to write the book, or fill in your questionaire?!
Annie (*shouting*) Don't you take that sarcastic tone to me! You tell me what
happens! (*She hovers over him, terrible violence in her eyes*)
Paul If you cut anything else off me I'll die. It won't be the shock of the
amputation, either, I'll... *I'll die on purpose!* (*He laughs. Like a crazy man*)
I'm so sorry, Annie, but I've ... really got to put my foot down this time!

*And obscene though it is, she laughs as well. They laugh and laugh. She
suddenly hugs him in a grotesque display of affection*

Annie Oh Paul, I thought you were going to die after your operation. I did,
I did, you were barely breathing! I had to put the glucose drips back in your
arms again, and keep changing the bandages on your weepy stump. I'll
never get a medal for what I've done, though Lord knows I deserve one.
Paul (*coldly*) You won't change my mind, you know.

Act II, Scene 8

She pulls back immediately from the embrace

Annie Oh, and why would I ever try to change your mind about *anything*? A Mister Smart Guy like you who thinks for a living? All I ever did was pull you out of your wrecked car before you could freeze to death and splint your broken legs and give you medicine and take care of you and talk you into writing the best book you *ever* wrote! If that's crazy, take me to the asylum!

Paul You also cut off my fucking foot!

She slaps him around the face with impressive speed

Annie Don't you use that eff word around me! I was raised better, even if you weren't! You're lucky I didn't cut off your man-gland! (*She pauses*) I thought about it.

Paul I know, I know.

Annie I want the end and I want it now!

Paul Very very soon. Just a couple more chapters.

Annie One more chapter!

Paul All right. One more chapter. Tomorrow you'll find out everything.

Her anger disappears, and she suddenly looks at him with real tenderness

Annie Oh Paul. Poor darling. This is where you belong, you know.

Paul doesn't know whether to laugh or cry

Yes, it is. Everyone else has forgotten about you. Oh, there were a few lines in the newspapers last year, tucked away where nobody reads things, and a silly young cop came round and asked me if I'd seen anything.

Paul Someone came round!?

Annie Only right at the beginning. You were still unconscious. But what's happened since? Nothing. All your so-called friends seem to have forgotten about you.

Paul No, they haven't——

Annie Yes, they have, Paul. Just like everyone knew about Denver but they've forgotten and don't bother any more. People don't care, you see. Oh, they might say they do, and kick up an almighty humbuggy fuss at the time, but pretty soon they forget.

Paul (*near to tears*) Somebody's still looking for me!

Annie Who, Paul? Not the police. They have more pressing things than a missing drunk driver. Not your fancy New York agent. I don't think she's paid for any special search parties, I haven't heard any helicopters combing

50   Misery

the woods for you. She's got plenty of other writers. And there isn't
anybody else, is there? You don't have any friends. You're like me.

Paul I'm *nothing* like you!

Annie We're no good with other people.

Paul Speak for yourself.

Annie I'm speaking for both of us, Paul. I read the book jackets. Two
marriages ... and two failures. You tried to write that "great" novel so
everyone would admire you, and you failed that as well. Truth is, you've
failed at just about everything, apart from Misery.

It is the truth, and he has nothing to say. She strokes his hair tenderly

I've got your Dom Perignon for when you finish, like you always have. It
cost seventy-five dollars for one bottle, but Chuckie Yoder at the liquor
store said it's the best champagne in the world.

Paul (*with a bitter laugh*) Well, old Chuckie knows his champagne. There's,
uh, there's something else I'd like, if you've still got them.

Annie What?

Paul There were some cigarettes in my bag——

Annie Now you know those things are no good for you, Paul. They give you
cancer.

Paul (*laughing*) Would you say cancer is something I have to worry about?
We all know what happens when I type "The End", don't we, Annie?

Now it's her turn to stay silent

I just want that one cigarette. For the end. What do you say, Annie? Be a
sport.

Annie All right ... but before the champagne. I'm not drinking a seventy-
five dollar bottle of fizzy beer in a room full of poison.

Paul OK. Put it on the table tonight, so I can smoke it on my own.

Annie It's going to be a good end, isn't it?

Paul Oh, yes. It's going to be hot stuff.

*Annie smiles and walks out. Then, without any warning, she comes hurtling
back towards him. She looks tortured, like two people fighting for possession
of one person*

Annie I love you, Paul! You know that, don't you!?

Paul Yes! Yes!

Annie I love you! (*She screams at him in total torment and confusion*) I don't
feel real! I don't feel real! I don't feel real!

Black-out

Act II, Scene 9   51

SCENE 9

The same. Morning

The Lights come up on Paul's room, the hall and the kitchen

Paul is smiling as Annie comes in

Annie You're not working.
Paul That's right. I've stopped work and I'm not doing any more. You know what I've just typed, Annie?
Annie All I know is you're not working, Mister Man! And you promised me——

Paul pushes his wheelchair back from his desk

Paul Two words. (*He picks up a half-smoked cigarette and drags deeply on it*)
Annie The End? The End! (*She makes a grab for the manuscript*)

He holds it away from her, grinning

Paul No peeking.
Annie Oh Paul, you get a whole row of gold stars! Oh boy! Wait until you see this! I've not only got you champagne—I've got you caviar! A great big gooey pile of caviar! Wait here! (*She runs out, through the hall into the kitchen*)

As soon as she leaves the room, Paul puts the wastebin in the middle of the room. He starts screwing up the pages of the manuscript into balls and stuffing them in the wastebin

Meanwhile, Annie is preparing the caviar, taking it from the fridge and spooning it out on to two pieces of bread. She is so excited she can't do it fast enough

(*Shouting*) I don't even know if I like this stuff or not! You don't get anything for the money!

Paul grabs the matches from by his cigarette and lights one. His hands are shaking really badly as he tries to light the pile of papers

Meanwhile, Annie dips her finger in the caviar and tries some—pulls a face

Oh Paul! It's so rich it makes you want to throw up! I don't like it!

52   Misery

Paul finally has the wastebin burning. He waits until it's really ablaze, then he wheels back to the bed and unbuckles the belt around his trousers

Paul Oh Aa-nnn-eee! Time for your story!

She gets the bottle of Dom Perignon from the fridge, and fairly rips the wrapping off

Annie I'm coming! Hang on a minute!

Annie loads everything on the tray as Paul removes his belt and tucks it behind him in his wheelchair

Paul (*shouting*) Annie, it's just the best thing I've ever done! False modesty aside, I've got to say this end's not good—it's much better than good. It's *great*!

She races back with the tray

Too bad you'll never read it.

She enters his room and we go into stroboscope. Annie sees the book burning and for a moment she absolutely freezes, open mouthed, and stares. Goes dead. She takes a step back, like an animal afraid of fire. She drops the tray and the caviar and the champagne. And she screams, a terrible naked howl of betrayal

Annie NO!
Paul It's a little trick I learnt from you.
Annie You can't burn Misery! You can't!

As she steps forward and drops to her knees to put it out, Paul rams his wheelchair forward and throws himself on top of her, whipping his belt around her neck. Annie struggles and kicks and struggles like the devil. He slams her to the ground and pulls the belt tight, jamming his knee in her back

(*Choking*) You cockadoodie brat!

He jerks the belt tighter. She tries to crawl away under the bed but Paul crawls after her, strangling her, banging her head on the floor. She crawls a bit more, then falls, apparently dead, half under the bed. He punches her body and laughs madly. He finally stops and his hand snakes across the bed and he pulls another manuscript from under his pillow

Act II, Scene 10 53

Paul I beat you, you bitch! Those were the notes I burnt! I beat you! (*He waves it at her*) You got burnt! This is my real book! (*He crawls away from her, clutching the manuscript to his chest*) This is my real book. (*He slumps on the floor, lacking the strength to pull himself back up into his chair. He slowly gets his breath back. He starts to smile, clutching his book*) This is my book. This is my book.

He doesn't see Annie rise slowly behind him, covered in blood. He still doesn't see her as she suddenly grabs him around the throat with her last breath and——

Black-out

Scene 10

Applause breaks out

Twenty-eighth Annual Romantic Fiction Awards

In darkness, we hear Paul's amplified voice and the sound of a schooner at sea. The scene begins as a tape, then cross-mixes to Paul reading aloud from his book

Paul (*reading*) "'Mistu Boss Rory, is she … dead?' Hezekiah enquired in a trembling voice, as Rory carried Misery's limp body on to the bunk in the captain's cabin. (*Beat*) After all this, could God really be cruel enough to let Misery die? Once he would have denied such a possibility, but in the dark continent of Africa he had discovered that there was not just one god, but many, and some were more than cruel—they were insane. (*Beat*) If his Misery were truly dead, as he had come to fear, he intended to go up to the foredeck and throw himself over the rail. These wretched thoughts were suddenly interrupted by a harsh gasp from Hezekiah. 'Mistu Boss Rory! Mistu Boss Rory! Look at her eyes! Look at her eyes!' (*Beat*) Misery's eyes, that gorgeously delicate shade of cornflower blue, had fluttered open. For a moment Rory saw only puzzlement in those eyes … and then recognition dawned in them, and then love, and he felt gladness roar through his soul."

The Lights come up and we see Paul, wearing a smart suit and looking very relaxed as he closes Misery's Return *and waits for the applause to die down. Behind him is another giant cut-out of a book, only this time it's* Misery's Return, *and the background shows the stone idol and the Bourka Bee people*

54   Misery

in an African landscape. A banner across the book announces "No.1 Bestseller!" Paul holds his bronze rose

Thank you, thank you, not just for this award, but for everyone who sent cards and letters when I was in hospital. I've got the Doctors Hospital in Queens to thank for my new plastic foot, and I am *not* addicted to painkillers, as some newspapers have been suggesting recently. Well, not much, anyway. After the sales of *Misery's Return* I never need to write again, and to be quite honest, I'm not sure I will. But if I do, well, I've got a wonderful non-fiction idea.

Black-out

FURNITURE AND PROPERTY LIST

Further dressing may be added at the director's discretion

ACT I

Scene 1

On stage: Giant cut-out of a romantic novel, as described on page 1
Microphone
Large bronze award in the shape of a rose

Personal: **Paul:** little index card

Scene 2

On stage: Bedroom:
Small wooden bench
Glass jars
Combs of honey
Bed. *On it:* flowered coverlet
Intravenous drip, not connected up
Chair
Bedside dresser. *On it:* small shaded lamp, glass containing water. *In a drawer:* old soft leather briefcase containing typed manuscript
Wastebin

Hall:
Small table. *On it:* small shaded lamp, black telephone

Seen only in Act II
Small bookcase. *In it:* Misery books
Faded magazine and newspaper cuttings on wall
Big, glossy signed photograph of Paul on wall, in horrible cheap frame, with shattered glass

56 Misery

Seen only in Act II
BATHROOM:
Dangling light switch
Shelves piled high with drugs, including bottle of Novril

Seen only in Act II
KITCHEN:
Sweet foods
Unwashed plates
Metal mesh on back door
Cooker
Chest of drawers. *In one drawer:* huge kitchen knife
Fridge containing bottle of Dom Perignon, caviar, bread
Tray
Spoon
Small shaded lamp

Front door with large locks
Ring of keys on hook by front door

Personal: **Annie:** wrist-watch (worn throughout), capsules

SCENE 3

Set: Soup
Spoon

SCENE 4

Set: Bucket
Soapy rag

SCENE 5

On stage: As before

Off stage: Shopping bag containing paperback book (**Annie**)

SCENE 6

Set: Book
Packet of biscuits
Carton of chocolate milk

Furniture and Property List 57

During Black-out on page 14:

Strike: Packet of biscuits

Set: Various empty snack packets

SCENE 7

Re-set: Empty glass on bedside dresser

SCENE 8

Re-set: Glass of water

Set: Old metal barbecue containing stack of scrunched-up typed pages
Box of matches

SCENE 9

Strike: Barbecue
Box of matches

Set: Silver Christmas tree. *On it:* tiny lights
Tin "smoker" wrapped as present
Wheelchair, partly wrapped, with bow on backrest
Old ugly black typewriter wrapped as present
Typing paper wrapped as present

Personal: **Annie:** cracker whistle, chewed pencil

SCENE 10

Off stage: Paper (**Annie**)
Urinal (**Annie**)

Personal: **Annie:** handkerchief

58   Misery

ACT II

Scene 1

Re-set: Bed

Set: Large, sticky beehive hanging in tree
               Table
               Small sheaf of papers

Strike: Christmas tree
               Gift wrappings

Scene 2

On stage: As before

Personal: **Paul:** bottle of pills

Scene 3

Set: Jar containing honey
               Knife

Scene 4

Off stage: Little rubber rat, dangling from small wooden trap (**Annie**)

Scene 5

On stage: As before

Scene 6

Re-set: Glass of water

Set: Trolley. *On it:* powerful flashlight
               Cotton wool swab
               Hypodermic needle
               Kitchen knife
               Small propane torch
               Matches
               Massive, rusty axe

Furniture and Property List

59

Fake blood
Dummy foot
Yellow floor bucket

SCENE 7

Set: Fresh flowers on table
Radio on **Paul**'s desk

SCENE 8

On stage: As before

SCENE 9

Set: Half-smoked cigarette
2 manuscripts, one under pillow on **Paul**'s bed
Matches

Personal: **Paul:** belt
Annie: fake blood

SCENE 10

On stage: Giant cut-out of a romantic novel, as described on page 54
Large bronze award in the shape of a rose

LIGHTING PLOT

Property fittings required: 4 pendant lights, wall brackets. Practical fittings required: 3 small shaded lamps, Christmas tree lights, flashlight
Composite setting

ACT I, SCENE 1

To open: Overall general lighting

Cue 1   **Paul** stands in front of microphone   (Page 1)
Flashbulbs flashing continuously

ACT I, SCENE 2

To open: Blinding car headlamps, replaced by snow effect and soft dawn light on **Paul**'s room

Cue 2   **Annie** "Whoink! Whoink! Whoink! Whoink!"   (Page 7)
Fade to darkness

ACT I, SCENE 3

To open: Turn on shaded lamps in Paul's room

Cue 3   **Paul**: "You're not mad at me, are you, Annie?"   (Page 9)
After a pause, slowly fade lights to darkness

ACT I, SCENE 4

To open: Single naked bulb in hall

Cue 4   **Annie** plays with the lights   (Page 9)
*Turn hall light on and off five times, then turn on main light on **Paul**'s room, as script page 9*

Cue 5   **Annie** turns out the light   (Page 11)
Snap main light off, replace with moonlight through trees

Lighting Plot 61

Cue 6	Sound of toilet flushing	(Page 11)
	After a pause, snap on lights in two tiny attic windows	

Cue 7	**Paul**: "Oh, Jesus Christ."	(Page 11)
	Black-out	

ACT I, SCENE 5

To open: Bright winter daylight in **Paul**'s room

Cue 8	**Annie**: "It's better."	(Page 13)
	Fade to darkness	

ACT I, SCENE 6

To open: Lights up on hall and **Paul**'s room. Snow effect outside

Cue 9	**Annie** drinks from carton of milk	(Page 14)
	After a pause, fade to darkness; after another pause,	
	slowly bring up lights on **Annie**	

Cue 10	**Annie** leaves, double locking front door	(Page 15)
	Slowly fade lights down	

ACT I, SCENE 7

To open: Darkness

Cue 11	**Paul** hears no answer to his call	(Page 16)
	Bring up dim lighting	

Cue 12	**Paul** sucks on the glass	(Page 16)
	Fade out lighting	

Cue 13	**Paul**: "...you bitch!"	(Page 16)
	Bring up dim lighting	

Cue 14	**Paul** starts crying	(Page 17)
	Fade light up and down continuously	

Cue 15	**Paul**: "...what these creative types are like!"	(Page 17)
	Start fading light down	

62   Misery

| *Cue* 16 | **Paul**: "…to drink your own piss…" | (Page 17) |

Fade to black-out

ACT I, SCENE 8

To open: Bring up glorious, blinding daylight in **Paul**'s room

| *Cue* 17 | **Annie** gives **Paul** tablets | (Page 20) |

Slowly fade lighting to black-out

ACT I, SCENE 9

To open: Snap on Christmas tree lights in **Paul**'s room

| *Cue* 18 | **Paul** turns on bathroom light | (Page 27) |

Snap on naked bulb in bathroom

| *Cue* 19 | **Paul** blacks out | (Page 27) |

Slowly fade out lighting

ACT I, SCENE 10

To open: Morning lighting in hall, bathroom and **Paul**'s room

| *Cue* 20 | **Paul** turns off bathroom light | (Page 28) |

Snap off bathroom light

| *Cue* 21 | **Paul** urinates | (Page 29) |

Slowly fade to black-out

ACT II, SCENE 1

To open: Spring day lighting in **Paul**'s room

| *Cue* 22 | **Annie**: "…enough of all your excuses." | (Page 32) |

Black-out

ACT II, SCENE 2

To open: Day lighting in **Paul**'s room

| *Cue* 23 | **Paul** starts typing again | (Page 33) |

Slowly fade to black-out

Lighting Plot 63

ACT II, SCENE 3

To open: Night lighting, shaded lamps on

Cue 24   **Paul** starts scribbling notes   (Page 36)
             Fade to black-out

ACT II, SCENE 4

To open: Dark, rainy day lighting, table lamp on in **Paul**'s room

Cue 25   Sounds of large schooner at sea   (Page 36)
             *Bring up outline of schooner's rigging, high in **Paul**'s
             room, moving in the wind*

Cue 26   **Annie**: "But mostly I just scream."   (Page 39)
             Black-out

ACT II, SCENE 5

To open: Night lighting in **Paul**'s room, the hall and kitchen

Cue 27   **Paul** wheels down the hall   (Page 39)
             Flash lightning on and off, continue sporadically

Cue 28   **Paul** turns on lamp in hall   (Page 39)
             Snap on lamp in hall

Cue 29   **Paul** enters kitchen   (Page 40)
             Illuminate kitchen with flashes of lightning

Cue 30   **Paul** brings out kitchen knife   (Page 40)
             Strong lightning directly overhead

Cue 31   **Paul** "It's the law of de jungle, Master Rory."   (Page 40)
             Big flash of lightning and black-out

ACT II, SCENE 6

To open: Darkness

Cue 32   **Paul**: "Oh, please don't!"   (Page 44)
             Flicker stroboscope light, continue

64   Misery

Cue 33   **Annie** spreads her legs like a logger   (Page 44)
            Decrease stroboscope flashes to one second in five

Cue 34   **Annie**: "Keep still! I must do this properly!"   (Page 45)
            Black-out for ten seconds, then flash; black-out for
            fifteen seconds, then flash

ACT II, Scene 7

To open: Glorious day lighting in **Paul**'s room

Cue 35   **Paul** starts typing again   (Page 46)
            Fade lighting down; bring up red light, faint outline
            of giant, hazy jungle sun on one side of stage

ACT II, Scene 8

To open: Night. Lights up on **Paul**'s room—red jungle sun as before

Cue 36   The sounds stop   (Page 47)
            Bring up ordinary lighting

Cue 37   **Annie**: "I don't feel real!" (third time)   (Page 50)
            Black-out

ACT II, Scene 9

To open: Overall morning lighting in **Paul**'s room, the hall and kitchen

Cue 38   **Annie** enters **Paul**'s room   (Page 52)
            Start stroboscope flicker

Cue 39   **Annie** grabs **Paul** by the throat   (Page 53)
            Black-out

ACT II, Scene 10

To open: Darkness

Cue 40   **Paul**: "...gladness roar through his soul."   (Page 53)
            Bring up lights

Cue 41   **Paul**: "...a wonderful non-fiction idea."   (Page 54)
            Black-out

EFFECTS PLOT

ACT I

Cue 1   **Paul** stands in front of microphone   (Page 1)
Huge applause

Cue 2   **Paul**: "Thank you."   (Page 1)
Fade out applause

Cue 3   **Paul**: "...have too much romance, do you?"   (Page 1)
Applause

Cue 4   **Paul**: "...I'll see you when the snow melts!"   (Page 2)
Applause

Cue 5   **Paul**: "...and my second divorce..."   (Page 2)
Laughter

Cue 6   **Paul**: "...what if Misery was a person?"   (Page 2)
Wild applause; after a pause, bring up low, ugly whine like car horn being pressed, louder and louder until it drowns applause; when ready cross-fade to gentle birdsong and sound of TV home shopping channel upstairs

Cue 7   **Annie** exits upstairs   (Page 11)
After a pause, sound of urinating followed by flush, upstairs

Cue 8   To open Scene 6   (Page 14)
Low sound of TV home shopping channel upstairs

Cue 9   Lights start to dim   (Page 15)
Footsteps in snow, then car driving off. Cut TV sound

Cue 10   **Paul**: "...if I don't get my Novril."   (Page 16-17)
Shifting music, continuing

66   Misery

Cue 11   To open Scene 9   (Page 20)
              Christmas carols, fade when ready

Cue 12   **Paul**: "…get me out of this."   (Page 26)
              Door slam, then car starting up and driving away

Cue 13   **Paul** starts to turn chair around   (Page 26)
              Sound of car approaching, getting louder, then fading away

Cue 14   To open Scene 10   (Page 27)
              *Sound of **Annie***'s car approaching, stopping, then footsteps*
                in snow, approaching, then keys in two locks

Cue 15   **Annie** pretends to look away   (Page 29)
              Jingle Bells *on radio next door*

ACT II

Cue 16   To open Scene 2   (Page 33)
              Sound like gun shot, then another, then several in rapid
                succession, machine gun scatter, then fade out under
              Paul*'s typing*

Cue 17   Lights begin to fade   (Page 33)
              *Amplify **Paul***'s typing, louder and louder*

Cue 18   To open Scene 3   (Page 33)
              Sound of wind outside, creaking from house and other
                farm buildings, continuing

Cue 19   **Paul**: "Her Ladyship rests not easy!"   (Page 34)
              Subtly mix in story sounds: barn owl, nails scratching wood

Cue 20   **Paul**: "…on that rotten Mr Griggor's toll gate." (Page 34)
              Very subtly mix in sound of pony and trap

Cue 21   **Paul**: "…outside the gates of the graveyard."   (Page 34)
              Mix in sounds of horses being pulled to a halt, footsteps
                racing across gravel footpath, then church bell tolling

Cue 22   **Paul** puts down the pages   (Page 35)
              Fade down wind sounds

Effects Plot

67

Cue 23	To open Scene 4 *Rain effect, continuing, then mix in sounds of large* *schooner at sea*	(Page 36)
Cue 24	**Annie** enters *Fade out schooner sounds*	(Page 37)
Cue 25	**Paul**: "…known as the Bee-People." *Fade up sounds of African port*	(Page 37)
Cue 26	Black-out *Amplify sound of rain*	(Page 39)
Cue 27	To open Scene 5 *Sounds of pouring rain, big thunder, frightened farm* *animals outside, continuing*	(Page 39)
Cue 28	Lightning directly overhead *Massive thunder*	(Page 40)
Cue 29	Big flash of lightning *Loud thunder*	(Page 40)
Cue 30	To open Scene 6 *Sound of trickle of water dripping off roof*	(Page 40)
Cue 31	**Annie**: "I'm a trained nurse!" *Music*	(Page 45)
Cue 32	To open Scene 7 *Music by Chopin on radio, bees in hive*	(Page 45)
Cue 33	**Paul** starts to type *Slow, ominous jungle drum beat, steady and doom-laden,* *joined by sound of bees, continuing*	(Page 46)
Cue 34	**Paul**: "…looked again on the dreadful sight." *Gradually amplify sound of bees and strengthen drum beat*	(Page 47)
Cue 35	**Paul** puts down the pages *Cut sound of bees and drums*	(Page 47)
Cue 36	Black-out *Applause, fade as Scene 10 begins*	(Page 53)

68   Misery

Cue 37   To open Scene 10   (Page 53)
            Paul's *amplified voice on tape and sound of schooner
            at sea, cross-mixing to* **Paul** *reading aloud*

Cue 38   **Paul**: "…roar through his soul."   (Page 53)
            Applause begins

Cue 39   **Paul** closes book   (Page 53)
            Fade out applause

A licence issued by Samuel French Ltd to perform this play does not include permission to use any Incidental music specified in this copy. Where the place of performance is already licensed by the PERFORMING RIGHT SOCIETY a return of the music used must be made to them. If the place of performance is not so licensed then application should be made to the Performing Right Society, 29 Berners Street, London W1.

A separate and additional licence from PHONOGRAPHIC PERFORMANCES LTD, 1 Upper James Street, London W1R 3HG is needed whenever commercial recordings are used.